STOP Marrying MISTAKES

PROVEN PRINCIPLES TO CLAIMING A HEALTHY RELATIONSHIP

LISA J. PECK

with DR. KEVIN B SKINNER, LMFT

MORGAN JAMES PUBLISHING • NEW YORK

Copyright ©2009 Lisa J. Peck

ISBN: 978-1-60037-522-4 (Paperback)
Library of Congress Control Number: 2008936945

Published by:

MORGAN · JAMES
THE ENTREPRENEURIAL PUBLISHER™
www.morganjamespublishing.com

Morgan James Publishing, LLC
1225 Franklin Ave Suite 325
Garden City, NY 11530-1693
Toll Free 800-485-4943
www.MorganJamesPublishing.com

Cover Design by:
James Arrington
www.pukrus.com

Interior Design by:
Rachel Lopez
rachel@r2cdesign.com

Habitat
for Humanity®
Peninsula
Building Partner

In an effort to support local communities, raise awareness and funds, Morgan James Publishing donates one percent of all book sales for the life of each book to Habitat for Humanity.

Get involved today, visit www.HelpHabitatForHumanity.org.

This book is dedicated to all the brave individuals who are courageously making their own lives and their children's lives better.

Acknowledgments

A special thanks to Dr. Kevin B. Skinner for his support and information that helped add richness to the book. Without Dr. Skinner asking me to write a divorce recovery book, *Stop Marrying Mistakes* would never have been written. Also thanks to Ken and Sharon Patey for their help and teaching through the years.

Contents

CHAPTER NINE

CHAPTER TEN

CHAPTER ELEVEN

CHAPTER TWELVE

CHAPTER THIRTEEN

CONCLUSION

CHARTS

Introduction

What do you say to a recently divorced person? "Congratulations!" "I'm sorry …" "What happened? "Can I still be friends with your ex?" Or "Who got the dog?" The answer depends on the situation, the people involved, and your relationship with them.

Face it, divorce is hard on everyone: the couple going through it, the neighbors, friends, associates, and maybe even the therapist. Working through the pain and designing an individualized springboard to rediscovered joy is what *Stop Marrying Mistakes* is all about. The tools, exercises, and principles found within these pages work. They have been put to the test and proven time after time.

Lisa J. Peck learned about Growth Climate and its education program when she was in the process of deciding whether or not to divorce her physically abusive husband, dealing with health issues, and raising six young children. Lisa took the leap. She traveled the emotional and physical maze from being a victim and finding herself trapped in a destructive relationship to enjoying life and exploring the freedom of creating more healthy relationships—not only with men but also with her children and friends.

What are the secrets that helped change not only the author's life but many others as well? This is what *Stop Marrying Mistakes* will teach you. It will show you not only to have more happiness in your life, but also how to pick up the pieces after divorce, how to effectively parent, how to be empowered and override depression, how to develop healthy relationships, and how and when to start dating, in addition to teaching you the tools for effective step-parenting and remarriage.

How to Use This Book

The intent of *Stop Marrying Mistakes* is to teach effective skills and offer tools that will make true healing possible, and if desired, assist with the selection of a future mate. The chapters in this book include stories, questions, and examples that will help those who find themselves single again navigate this challenging territory. Though there are many phases of divorce (e.g., going through the pain of a divorce, picking up the pieces, learning to believe in ourselves again, dating, remarriage), the goal of *Stop Marrying Mistakes* is to help you keep moving forward by starting from the stage you are in.

Since each divorce is unique, there may be some chapters that are more helpful than others. Nevertheless, all the questions are designed to help identify issues that you may need to deal with so that you can begin anew with clarity and happiness. Divorce is the end of a marriage, not the end of life. Joy can be found and experienced afterwards.

Divorce is the end of a marriage, not the end of life.

PICKING UP THE PIECES: HOW TO BEGIN THE HEALING PROCESS

On the day of my wedding, the howling wind woke me hours before the alarm. My sleep had been restless. Kicking the blanket off, I rose to catch a glimpse of the dark sky. Taking a deep breath, I parted my drapes to admire the last sparkle of stars before the sunlight disguised them from view.

That day I was taking steps in my life's journey that would permanently change my future. Dramatic changes were before me, and I could hardly wait to start.

Unlike many, I was not nervous on my wedding day. I had no need to be. I was marrying a man who loved me so much he couldn't hide his desire to make me his wife. We had met at a dance a mere two and a half months earlier and fell instantly in love. We just clicked. It felt as if I had gone home; which I thought at the time was a good thing. When he proposed, I was surprised that it came so soon but knew from his pleading eyes that to say no would crush him. I couldn't do that to him. As I hesitated, he described what our future would be like. We would develop our art, have beautiful children who would love us, and we would be happy. I believed him. Like most people, the thought that we would divorce never crossed my mind. Our love was strong, our commitment firm. Nothing would come between us.

The statistics that one out of every two couples divorce never penetrated my thoughts that early May morning as I looked out the window at the sky, thinking about my upcoming wedding. Yet thirteen years later I received the much anticipated phone call from my lawyer, "Congratulations, you're officially divorced."

After hanging up the phone, I wondered, "Now what?" What would I do now that my dream had been shattered into a million pieces? How was I going to go on? What would it take to put one foot in front of the other? How would I glue myself back together so I could dream, smile, laugh, and embrace life? It seemed, at the beginning, impossible to be happy again—to feel alive and okay.

> **How would I glue myself back together so I could dream, smile, laugh, and embrace life?**

But it's not impossible, and how to get there is what we're going to explore.

How would I glue myself back together so I could dream, smile, laugh, and embrace life?

Picking Up the Pieces—Are You Ready?

Okay, now you are officially divorced. If you're anything like me, when the announcement came it was a shock. Yes, I fought with my future ex over the big screen TV, the dog, the house, the children, and a thousand times I whispered that I couldn't wait for the whole mess to be over. The reality that I was actually going to be a *divorced person* never completely registered in my mind. Once those documents were signed and the judge put his John Hancock on the dotted line, *boom*, I found myself on a very different journey than I had traveled as a married person. What to do?

"Heal" is a message that divorced people hear a lot. I would be a millionaire if I were paid a dollar every time someone told me, "You've got to give yourself time to heal." Great. I'd love to heal. I have a life I want to get on with, so let's do it. But how?

Before you can fix something, you have to know what the problem is. So despite the fact that it's not fun to look at the truth of our wounded lives, it is important to be thorough and honest when doing so. If you're not, you're only cheating yourself.

Exercises to Assist in Healing

Take a few minutes now to think about what you've already gotten through since the day your divorce was finalized.

In the assignment below you will be asked to identify some of the most challenging things you have had to deal with since your divorce. Do it. Grab a pen and honestly answer the questions. Remember: the more honest you are with yourself, the faster you'll heal and the sooner you'll be relieved of pain. Additionally, the more honest you are now, the faster you'll develop the necessary skills to form a healthy lifestyle. So what are you waiting for? Let's start.

Before you can fix something, you have to know what the problem is.

ASSIGNMENT 1: What are the five most difficult things you have had to deal with as a direct result of your divorce? Write down how each of these has impacted you, your children, and others.

1)

Impact on me:

Impact on my children:

Impact on others:

2)

    Impact on me:

    Impact on my children:

    Impact on others:

3)

    Impact on me:

    Impact on my children:

    Impact on others:

4)

    Impact on me:

    Impact on my children:

    Impact on others:

5)

Impact on me:

Impact on my children:

Impact on others:

How to Create a New Climate Where You Can Grow and Develop

Now that you have listed some of the core challenges that have impacted you, it's time to evaluate your current climate so you can identify the issues that are preventing you from moving forward. Every place, every person, every relationship has a climate. A climate is a prevailing temper, trend, or condition. In order for human relations to grow and develop, it's necessary to have a safe climate where thoughts, ideas, goals, and aspirations can be shared. The environment in which you find yourself impacts your state of mind. For example, have you ever walked through a messy kitchen where your foot got stuck on sticky stuff with each step? Stepping on sticky stuff will affect your thinking and feelings not only about the kitchen, but also about others you live with and life in general. This experience is totally different when the house is freshly clean and you know where everything is. A clean or dirty kitchen can affect the way you think and feel in positive and negative ways. The same principle applies to human development. It responds to both negative and positive environments.

Most human development occurs in a safe climate. This means that if you want to grow and change, you need to understand how to establish and use a few fundamental rules that will help you enjoy your healthy relationship for growth and shape it for growth.

The First Fundamental Rule of Growth: Understanding Your Own Climate—You Have a Story

People can create a safe climate within themselves. Consider meditation: The objective of meditation is to help a person find the place where an inner climate of peace resides. If we can find that place of inner peace, the inner-self is nurtured from the inside out.

The following three assignments are designed to help you identify your inner climate. Take your time and seriously consider the implications of your answers. It has been my experience that in the early stages of divorce it is hard to find peace. If this is the case for you, I recommend you focus on the assignment.

Finding peace in your life begins with finding peace with yourself.

ASSIGNMENT 2A: How often do you feel at peace with yourself? Circle the answer that best describes your current feelings.

a. Daily

b. 3–5 times a week

c. Once a week

d. 2–3 times a month

e. Seldom

ASSIGNMENT 2B: Explain your answer from above. Write down the last time you felt inner peace. Describe the type of climate you were in when you felt it. Include where you were, who you were with, why you were there, what time of day it was, and your purpose for being there. If you can't remember a time, describe what you think it would look like, feel like, and be like. What feelings would you have?

ASSIGNMENT 3: Make a list of things you can do to create a safe climate for yourself. They don't have to be hard. It could be as simple as taking a hot bath or appreciating the sunrise as you drive to work. After you construct the list, go back through and pick at least three things that you're going to start doing immediately to create a safe climate. Once you have picked three, write when you're going to make them happen. Be specific: say Tuesday at 7:30 a.m. This lodges the information in your mind. Put this appointment with yourself in your calendar and schedule it.

Taking time for yourself is an important part of creating a safe climate. This builds trust within yourself that you will do what you say to keep yourself healthy, grounded, and safe.

If you make a commitment that you're going to start doing things to keep yourself safe, you need to honor and keep that commitment, or you will not trust yourself.

The Second Fundamental Rule of Growth:
Our Behavior Affects the Climate in Our Relationships

Sometimes it's difficult to assess how our behaviors affect the climate of our relationships with others. What each of us talks about significantly impacts what others around us feel and think. If you would like an example of this, consider how you felt the last time someone told you bad news. Their information probably had a direct impact on your mood and how you felt inside. What we do can affect what others around us feel. For example, when parents are going through a divorce, their children are observing a lot of stress and tension in their caregivers.

The thing about divorce is that you have a story. Most people, including the cats and dogs, want to know why. "What happened?" and "Did he/she really…?" are the common questions you will get. As you tell your story, this is the climate you are presenting to others.

A vindictive climate will often push people away. While you may have anger, these approaches will not help you heal nor will they allow you to create healthy relationships.

So what exactly is your story? What are you telling others? A person's story may go something like this: My wife was impossible to live with. She had to keep a spotless house. I would get up to go to the bathroom in the middle of the night and she would make the bed. She took the spoon out of my mouth when I was eating to put it in the dishwasher. She was such a clean freak—completely impossible. I'm sure lucky to be away from her.

"Oh, he is such a slob. He leaves his socks, pants—you name it—on the floor. He's so lazy and just wants to play. He never works. Good riddance to the bum."

Your story may sound like this or may be something very different. "It was all her fault." "It was all his fault." "It was all my fault. I'm so stupid." No matter what your story is, it is important to know it. You go through the tale in your head on a regular basis. You must also observe how your story is understood or misunderstood by others.

Now it is time to examine your story and see how it works for you. Are you the victim? Are you the one who survived? Or can you see where both of you could have done things differently?

No matter what your story is, it is important to know it.

In this section you will be asked to determine how your story of the divorce influences the people around you. An added bonus will be that once you see how it affects others, you may see on a deeper level how it impacts you.

As you think about your story, it will have an impact on your emotions. You may get upset, irritated, sad, or you may feel relieved. These emotions turn into thoughts that create the climate inside of you. Your mind requires that you make meaning out of your divorce. Let's see what your mind did with your experience.

ASSIGNMENT 4A: Take some time to write down the story you tell others about your divorce. What did you say? How did you describe the break-up?

ASSIGNMENT 4B: How did the individuals to whom you told your story respond? Did their response surprise you? Or was it predictable?

ASSIGNMENT 4C: Describe the effect their response had on YOU. Did it make you feel justified? Guilty? Pleased? Angry?

Now that you have gone in depth, looked at your stories, and considered how they affect you and others, your awareness of the power of what you say will stay with you as you put together more stories to tell in the future.

The Third Fundamental Rule of Growth:
The Climate or Mood of Individuals around You Has
a Profound Effect on You

Most of the time you aren't even aware of how deeply a climate is affecting you.

After my husband left the house (okay, was escorted out by the police), something amazing began to happen. At first I was overwhelmed with what being separated meant: the children, the financial problems, the fights, and the judgment by others. Plus, I was filled with the fear of being on my own. But within a day or two, my friends noticed that the stress lines on my face had lessened and I was starting to have fun. The more space and time I spent away from my husband, the more I found myself relaxing and becoming a more carefree, happy person—probably more of the person I really was, but always had to hide.

The experience of feeling so alive and free once one is separated from a spouse who is less than a positive influence is common. Many people go through feelings of relief and freedom when they are no longer around a toxic boss, parent, child, neighbor, or friend. This relief and freedom can come as an enormous surprise, but it shows just how much being around a negative drain can not only affect our thoughts but also our psyches and even our very souls. When an individual is in a constant state of stress, he or she often goes into a state of survival rather than achievement and creativity.

> **In order for a person to grow, a safe emotional and psychological climate needs to be present.**

If you're not in a safe situation, your mind constructs devices to protect you. Although each construct is written with a different instruction manual, the overall purpose is to lock down resources and simply survive. In such a mental state, there is little room for growth, and the ability to learn new things is severely hampered. There have been remarkable stories, however, of people who have not only survived but thrived in terrible situations: Viktor Frankl's *Man's Search for Meaning* is one. While in a Nazi war camp, he realized that his life depended on his ability to create a personal environment of hope until escape was possible. In order for a person to grow, a safe emotional and psychological climate needs to be present. So you see, no matter how bad things get, growth truly is dependent upon a certain state of mind.

If you want to assess the climate around you, begin with yourself, and then evaluate the external climate. The following information will help you survey your internal and external climates.

During a divorce, the climate surrounding others may make it difficult to find peace. This is especially true if your ex-spouse, children, relatives, or clergy suggest there is something wrong with you. It has been my experience that individuals who have been through a divorce worry about how others perceive them.

To add to this problem, many people are not discreet with their judgments. A friend told me about an experience she had that is common for many divorcées. She struggled to go to church because as she walked down the hall people either stopped talking and stared or turned away and whispered.

Individuals who have been through a divorce worry about how others perceive them.

When these things happen, it is natural to feel that others are looking down on you and condemning you. You might begin to isolate yourself to avoid judgment. If you hide from life, happiness and the pleasure life can offer will not be able to find you. Isolating oneself in a depressed or guilty state is dangerous and not advised. While contemplation and meditation can help, remember that isolation in a depressed mood is much different from solitude and the joy and insight solitude can offer.

> **Individuals who have been through a divorce worry about how others perceive them.**

Another part of understanding one's external climate comes in identifying how often we feel compelled to defend ourselves against the judgments of others. The problem is that when we constantly defend ourselves, we don't have time or energy to create, set goals, or accomplish ordinary tasks. Basically, we get so worried about what everyone else thinks that we aren't engaged in life.

Even more importantly, defending ourselves and the role that we played in the marriage keeps us trapped in that marriage. It's more productive to resolve the past, let it go, and create a new here and now. This cannot happen if we're constantly fighting battles against a real or imagined foe.

Defending ourselves and the role that we played in the marriage keeps us trapped in that marriage.

It is important to understand what you feel is happening around you and the people in your outer world. These influences can feel like weights that drain your energy and hold you back from healing. Becoming aware of who is present in your life right now and how their presence impacts you will help you to heal faster.

Defending ourselves and the role that we played in the marriage keeps us trapped in that marriage.

The next assignment will help you assess the external influences or climate that may be slowing down your efforts to walk the path of healing. As with the other assignments, it's important to write the answers down. If you just think about the answers without putting them to pen and paper, you'll miss much of the benefit.

ASSIGNMENT 5A: Identify the climate you feel surrounds the individuals listed below.

Your ex-spouse or soon-to-be ex-spouse

Your children (if you have children)

Your family

Your out-laws or in-laws

Clergy or religious leader

Mutual friends: yours and your ex-spouse's

Your friends

Your coworkers

Neighbors

Others

ASSIGNMENT 5B: What type of climate do you feel is created inside you when you're around or associate with the following individuals?

1. Your ex-spouse or soon-to-be ex-spouse

2. Your children (if you have children)

3. Your family

4. Your out-laws or in-laws

5. Clergy or religious leader

6. Mutual friends: yours and your ex-spouse

7. Your friends

8. Your co-workers

9. Neighbors

10. Others

The Fourth Fundamental Rule of Growth:
Understand How to Discover Your Inner Strengths and the
Support System around You

Up to this point we have assessed your internal climate and external climate. Now we move on to how to determine resources in the climate around you. If you have a hard time trusting others, start with your own internal resources and then look outward. Here are a few observations that may help you.

How to Use Your Internal and External Resources

I have observed many people going through divorces and have been fascinated by the significant differences in how people react. Some individuals respond better than others.

I wondered what created such differences. The first answer was obvious. The belief people had in themselves often determined how well they did. Sometimes even those who possessed a high confidence became worn down from depression and had to struggle to go on. Even more puzzling, some who had a lower self-esteem did much better. They were better able to keep their spirits up and were more functional. Why?

I discovered that the people who did much better through this difficult time in their lives were those individuals who had a support system. Those with family, clergy, friends, or other social support had higher spirits and more hope that they would make it through the despair and reclaim joy in their lives. This observation led me to conclude that one of the key elements to making it through any divorce or loss is having the support of loved ones.

Another key element that I observed in people who did well after divorce was that they had a strong inner commitment to discovering and reinforcing their strengths. They worked to identify their personal strengths and used those strengths to help them move on. True healing requires work. The more time and effort put into your healing, the sooner you will feel comfortable with your life.

Resources begin with your own. Understanding your core feeds your own support systems. Taking into account the resources available to you from inside yourself and from others will provide you with perspective and strength beyond what you originally thought was available.

The assignments in this section are designed to help you identify the internal and external resources that you have available, even if you don't think you have any.

ASSIGNMENT 6A: What are your greatest talents and strengths? Identify as many as you can. See if you can think of up to twenty. If you are convinced that you don't have any more or feel too depressed to think of more, ask someone close to you who you trust to be sensitive and honest, and ask them to complete your list with you.

For example:

Kind

Trustworthy

Friendly

Honest

Smart

Sense of humor

Creativity

Good at discernment

Patient

Forgiving

1

2

3

4

5

6

7

8

9

10

11

12

13

14

15

16

17

18

19

20

To assist you with confirming your strengths, go online to www.stopmarrying mistakes.com. There you'll find the **Strengths Summary Form,** a fill-in-the-blank form that can highlight your strengths. Print and post it on your wall to be a daily reminder.

Knowing your strengths and reviewing them is a powerful tool to counter the discouragement you face on the low days. A lot of times people who have gone through a divorce have had their weakness, or what their former spouse thought of as their weakness, pointed out many times. It's time to rid your mind of the negative naysayer and plug into your awareness of the things that you're good at.

ASSIGNMENT 6B: Review the list of strengths in 6a and identify how these strengths could help you move forward. Be specific. Next write an action plan on how you will use those strengths to help you navigate through upcoming problems.

1

2

3

4

5

6

7

8

9

10

ACTION PLAN:

Picking up the pieces and starting a new life can be frustrating and overwhelming at times, but it can also be a rewarding experience that can enrich and bless your life. In order to be successful in this endeavor, become aware of yourself, how you affect others and how they affect you. This is an important step. This awareness is exciting because it means that you can change some things and create a life that works better for you and those you love.

HOW TO FEEL AGAIN

F eeling whole is never easy. After a divorce, it may seem even more challenging. Sometimes, on an extremely bad day, it may seem impossible. Most of the parts you liked about your life when you were married are gone. A lot of divorced people no longer see their children every day or the friends that they once enjoyed with their former spouse. They have had to move out of, and possibly sell, the home they spent time building, fixing, or decorating. Alternatively, it could be painful to remain in the home with its memories.

3 Crucial Steps to Heal

Crucial Step 1: Mourn the Loss

Some say that divorce is much harder than the death of a spouse. The reasoning behind this theory is that the person is going through a similar loss and change of life but isn't allowed the socially and culturally accepted grieving process. Plus, there's no life insurance policy, and there is often staggering debt. Think about it: If we lose the love of our life in death, no one expects us to be functional for quite some time. People say to one another, "His/Her spouse has died." That seems to explain everything. Some cultures even give the individual a set time period where they are in official mourning. If, on the other hand, an individual is going through a divorce and acting depressed, the chances are much higher that a critical eyebrow will be raised. For some reason, the recently divorced are magically expected to go on as if they only hit a bump in the road.

> Some say that divorce is much harder than the death of a spouse.

Those who lose their spouses to death are more often left to mourn with cherished memories, which can be comforting. Those who lose their spouses to divorce are more often left with bitter experiences that need to be sorted through and resolved differently.

The adjustment to singlehood can be especially difficult on women who lack the basic maintenance skills such as car repair, house repair, mowing, weeding, and financial management. Learning such skills when one is already emotionally exhausted can be overwhelming. Some face another steep mountain that must be climbed with the now critical need of supporting themselves. This can be daunting if the newly divorced individual has no concrete, marketable skills. The stress only grows when this person has live-in dependents.

Whether you have lost your spouse to death or divorce, it is absolutely necessary to mourn the loss. Until this step is taken, it will be virtually impossible to move on. In order to heal, you must realize how the loss has impacted your life.

All this stress and loss must be respected. When you are first going through a divorce, slow down your lifestyle to get more sleep, rest, and time to cry. The tears and screams all need to come out. Respect this time as if you were someone who lost your spouse to a terminal illness. Give yourself time to just be. Rest. Be angry. This is critical in moving forward. The feelings are not going to go away. If you pretend they aren't there and try to push forward with your life, they will catch up with you. There is no escaping the pain.

One of the best ways to deal with your pain is to write, write, write. It's not enough to think it in your head. There's something about pen and paper connecting that draws the truth out. Writing out your answers and feelings can be very healing.

If you pretend the feelings aren't there and try to push forward with your life, they will catch up with you.

ASSIGNMENT 7: Make a list of the things you may need to mourn due to your divorce.

EXAMPLE: I need to mourn the loss of my dreams. All I wanted was a spouse who would love our children and me. I need to mourn that loss.

Or write a letter saying goodbye to everything that you thought you would have. Here is an example of what this letter, taken from the novel *Silent Cries*, could look like.

Goodbye,

Goodbye, dear house that I never wanted to move into. I was so scared the first night behind your walls, feeling everyone was peeking in. But I learned to love you, to make you my own. I spent hours decorating and recreating so I would find my own identity and I could settle in.

I loved my sitting room with my beautiful couch and wall hanging, my office with a view and the quick exit door to the playground where I played with my baby, Nathan. I never made you complete, but I was on my way.

Goodbye dear house with the memories. The holes in the walls, the busted doors, the roof I escaped to, climbing up while eight and half months pregnant. Goodbye to the spot where the TV sat and where he threw the remote control and bruised my womb that carried our youngest son. Goodbye to the bedroom where I tried to wake him up to go to the hospital because my water broke with my last baby. He wouldn't take me for hours. Goodbye to the bed where I was attacked in my sleep.

Goodbye to my library lined with books, one of the places I would flee to, hide from him; to my office where I called out for help so many times while he banged on the door or went searching for the key.

Goodbye to my bathroom, which I made my "mini-Hawaii," but where he also busted the door. Goodbye to him owning me. Goodbye to the sweet words "my husband," to the feeling I belonged to someone and was wanted. Goodbye to the hope that he'd make good on all his promises, the promises that said he was there for me and cared for me. Goodbye to the promise that he'd love me. Goodbye to the belief that he'd ever give empathy.

Goodbye to his malicious verbal attacks, to his physical abuse, to objects flying at me, especially in the middle of the night when he'd keep me up. Goodbye to the hours of intense ridicule. Goodbye to the triangulation with the kids. Goodbye to being talked out of trusting my instincts. Goodbye to fear. Goodbye to never being good enough. Goodbye to an unhappy marriage and to the constant effort of trying to be better and thinking something is wrong with me. Goodbye to poor health, because now I am free to be myself and to do my emotional work.

Goodbye to the neighbors who were never my friends and who never accepted me. Goodbye to the gym three minutes away, to Carla so close and therapy around the corner.

Goodbye to Brad's broad chest that I always believed would protect and keep me safe. Goodbye to unendurable intensity. Goodbye to his talk-it-to-

death antics. Goodbye to his cruel comparisons to my parents. Goodbye to his beliefs that my thoughts, beliefs, and feelings aren't valid. Goodbye to my effort in helping him heal.

Goodbye to not having friends because he chased them away. Goodbye to my anger that kept me safe from him because it helped me have the courage to say no.

Goodbye.........Hello, FREEDOM!!!!!!

Go to **Goodbye Letter Form** *link at www.stopmarryingmistakes.com. There you'll find a* **Good-bye Letter Form** *with prompts that will assist you. Writing the letter releases your grief resulting from the break-up of your relationship.*

One of the biggest tasks after divorce is to identify the impact your divorce has had on you. Have you ever had an open wound that needed to be cleaned out before you put on the bandage? Imagine having a deep wound filled with dirt, and instead of cleaning it you put on a bandage. Many people do this when they go through a divorce. They refuse to notice the dirt or clean it away. Consequently, the unresolved issues cause tremendous infection and pain. The assignment below will help you identify areas in which your divorce has impacted you.

ASSIGNMENT 8A: Make a list of the relationships that have been impacted the most by your divorce (e.g. work, personal confidence, your relationships with your children, your former in-laws, the neighbors, your friends, your own family, your finances, etc.). Write them down and be specific.

1

2

3

4

5

6

7

8

9

10

Assignment 8b: After you write about how the divorce has affected your relationships with others, it's time to get closer and examine how your divorce has affected your relationship with yourself. What did you think of yourself before the divorce? What do you think of yourself now? What has changed? If your viewpoint is more negative, can you think of a way to reframe your thoughts?

Crucial Step 2: Nourish Your Mind and Body

Divorce is one of the most challenging events a person may ever experience mentally, emotionally, and physically. Unfortunately, during and after a divorce, many people stop doing the basic things that keep them healthy. If you want to improve your chances of staying emotionally and physically fit, consider doing the basics—eating, exercising, and getting adequate sleep. Your mind functions much better and more positively when it is cared for. Researchers have repeatedly found that individuals who eat well, exercise, and get regular sleep (7–9 hours a night) function better day-to-day.

Often after going through something like a divorce, people cop the attitude, "Why should I?" "What's there to live for?" "I don't want to do anything but stay in bed." If you're harboring these thoughts or anything similar, recognize that such thoughts come from depression. One of the best ways to beat depression is staying away from sweets, getting enough sleep, and exercising, which increases the healthy endorphins.

Unfortunately, during and after a divorce, many people stop doing the basic things that keep them healthy.

Eating

To let you know that you are normal, if you struggle in this area, I will share what I went through, and how I managed to get a grip on my life. I had a hard time taking care of myself after my divorce. I did great: eating lots of veggies, going to the gym, and sleeping at least a couple of hours a night when my children were with me. But when my ex would come and whisk them away for the weekend, my slippery slope would begin.

I ate and took care of myself most of the weekend that they were gone. Well let me clarify—I took care of myself when I was at events, meeting people, and socializing, but when the events weren't happening and I was taking a break from work, my descent began.

Time passed; the quiet transformed gradually from welcome relief into loneliness. I longed to be with my children when they weren't there. I began to struggle more with eating. Why cook? There was only me. It had never been only me. I came from a large family, and making dinner for one person seemed an utter waste of time.

I am hypoglycemic, and going without food can cause serious problems. It didn't take long for me to notice my pattern. By Sunday night, when the kids returned, I was too weak to greet them. These habits didn't serve them or me.

To solve this problem, I had to acknowledge that I didn't do well without my children. I needed support and a game plan to help me through those times. I called my divorced friend next door and opened up to him about my struggles. As a solution, we decided that we would eat Sunday dinner together. We would see how healthy we could make the experience. He was trying to become more health conscious. This turned into fun weekly dinners that not only made that last little bit without my children easier on me but also blessed his life. When I left to go home to greet my children, he would have a big grin on his face. He'd say, "Thank you for the leftovers. I'll enjoy them for lunch tomorrow."

After he understood my problem, he would call me on Sunday mornings to make sure I had eaten and wouldn't get off the phone until I had. As time progressed, I adapted to being on my own and without my children. I no longer needed him to call me, but we kept cooking the dinners together because we both ate better—and it was fun.

My problem was under eating. Others may have problems with overeating. No matter which way one copes, both are unhealthy. Pulling together with other singles can be a solution.

No matter what your unique struggles are after you're divorced, it's important to recognize your specific problems. You can't solve what you don't acknowledge. Once you have a clear picture of your patterns, look for ways you can overcome them. Be creative. There is more than one answer, and there is a solution that fits perfectly for you.

Below is an assignment that will help you discover creative ways to address your own issues and concerns.

ASSIGNMENT 9A: Monitor your eating habits for at least one week. Are you eating regularly? Do you eat healthy foods (daily food groups)? If yes, continue on— if no, take time and make specific goals to improve your eating habits. Now look at your goals and come up with a surefire way you can be successful. Do whatever it takes to make sure you will make it. Join one of the weight assistance programs where there are people you have to report to. Ask your best friend to help you. It doesn't matter how you do it, just make sure you can't weasel out of your goals when times get harder. Set up the support system that will work best for you.

To assist you monitoring your eating go online to www.stopmarryingmistakes.com and download your weekly eating chart.

Exercise

Most people know the benefits of exercise so we won't go into most of them. But one we will focus on is that exercise is the great deterrent of depression. It releases chemicals that act much like an antidepressant. With all the unpleasantness a divorce entails, it becomes important to assist your body as much as possible.

With all the unpleasantness divorce entails, it becomes important to assist your body as much as possible.

Many divorcées that I know struggle with frequent sickness. Why? Their bodies are worn-out from the increased stress that comes with the process of divorce, and their immune system wears down. Being ill magnifies your problems.

It's important to release the tension, and exercise can help. There are other advantages to exercising when you are single. For instance, there are more opportunities that might make exercise fun for you. Many singles meet as a group to enjoy various sports— hiking, rock climbing, basketball, dancing, etc. If you join one of these groups, you are getting more involved in life, exercising, and having fun. You don't have to be ready to date either. Many people participate for the friendship and love of the sport. If you want to meet others to possibly date, of course these groups are a great way of finding people who enjoy similar things. Some groups are all-male and some are all-female. It depends on what you're looking for. There are so many things out there. Many groups are completely free. Search until you find one (or several) that best fit your needs. You can locate these groups in the newspaper, on the Internet, through different Internet dating services, by word-of-mouth, or through a therapist.

Another fun place to go for exercise is the gym, if you can afford it. There are many singles out there, and exercising with others makes it more fun instead of drudgery. You can also exercise with a friend. Call your neighbors until you find someone with similar goals, and exercise together. Choose something that works for you. Pick something that seems more like fun than a "have to" and you will be feeling better in no time.

ASSIGNMENT 10: Monitor your exercise habits for at least one week. Are you exercising 3 to 5 times a week? If yes, continue on—if no, take time and make specific goals to get more exercise.

To assist you monitoring your exercise habits go online to www.stopmarrying mistakes.com and download your weekly exercise chart.

Sleep

As every parent knows, one of the best solutions for an ornery child who thinks life is terrible and nothing will get better is to get him or her to sleep. When a person is rested, the whole world seems like a different place. It's the same for adults, but somehow we think we can slide around the issue. Truthfully, we can't. How often do you fall asleep in a meeting or while driving? How often do you feel tired, fatigued, and wish you had more energy?

When stress hits, the need for sleep increases dramatically. Often, someone going through a divorce struggles with sleep. For some, being alone at night can cause increased anxiety. If you experience nervous energy at night, there are things you can do. Here are some hints.

Helping Sleep Come

DRINK CHAMOMILE TEA OR SLEEP ENHANCING HERBAL TEA.
Chamomile is great for calming nerves and slowing your racing thoughts. Use two tea bags, and most of the time it's impossible to stay awake.

LISTEN TO RELAXING MUSIC. This is soothing and relieves feelings of loneliness. It also calms the anxiety that every divorced person goes through as they wonder what lies ahead.

MEDITATION. There are some great meditations that help slow the brain and allow sleep to come. Here's a great exercise: lie down and breathe naturally. Start from your feet and release the tension in the muscles. Breathe out the stress and slowly let your attention drift up toward the scalp. There are also great meditation tapes that utilize music and instructions.

CUT OUT THE SUGAR. It may be bad news, but sugar can keep you awake. Cut out sugar completely from your diet for a week, and you will be surprised at many of the health results. After you're convinced that it does make a difference in your sleep and overall health, you determine how much sugar you can handle without it affecting your sleep or other health considerations.

Some newly separated people have a hard time sleeping in an empty bed. To solve this problem, one single man gathered up pillows and put them against his back so it felt like someone else was in the bed. This helped until he grew accustomed to being alone.

Understanding your own sleeping patterns and how they have changed after your divorce can help you to feel better and more involved in your life. Use the following exercise to evaluate how well you are sleeping and supporting your overall good health and happiness.

ASSIGNMENT 11: Monitor your sleeping patterns for at least one week. Do you have a regular sleep pattern? Are you getting seven to nine hours of daily sleep? If yes, good for you, continue on—if no, take time and make goals on things you can do to improve your sleeping habits.

To assist you monitoring your sleep go online to www.stopmarryingmistakes. com and download your weekly sleep chart.

Crucial Step 3: Evaluate Your Aspirations and Passions

Some people get the mistaken idea that because they are divorced their chance to live the life they dreamed of is over.

Everyone needs hopes and dreams—they make life worth living. Some people get the mistaken idea that because they are divorced their chance to live the life they dreamed of is over. Wrong! Yes, your greatest dream might have been to have the perfect marriage, to have delightful kids who aren't shuffled back and forth, to never again suffer loneliness, and all those other things newly married people promise themselves. True, maybe these visions will never happen, but you can transform your dream, change it, and create more happiness and success than what you might have ever been capable of having if your marriage had not dissolved.

Once you get through the initial difficult transition, you'll have more reason to believe that you have better things to look forward to. After all, you just unhitched yourself from a bad relationship that was causing you enough frustration to lead you to terminate it.

When I spoke with a therapist friend, he reiterated the following story to me: One of my patients got divorced. She thought she was now destined to be an old maid forever and would live a life of isolation and loneliness. This made her sad, but it was preferable to staying in such a miserable situation in her marriage. What she didn't realize until after she was divorced and had made adjustments was that divorce wasn't the end. It was a new beginning. Now that she was out of an unworkable situation, she didn't have to use her energy trying to make an extremely difficult relationship work. She could focus on other things.

Divorce is a new start, a clean slate. You can create any life that you want. From the point of the divorce onward, you're responsible for how your life turns out. You can mope and be depressed. You

> **From the point of the divorce onward, you're responsible for how your life turns out.**

can constantly reflect on what could have been. Or you can assess what happened, change the things about yourself that you want to change, and start masterminding goals for the future.

The following assignment will help you understand how to make your hopes and dreams come true.

ASSIGNMENT 12A: Think back to an earlier time in your life and assess what your hopes, dreams, and aspirations were. If you are struggling to think of something, ask for help. Are your parents around or a childhood friend? Ask them if they can remember what you talked about doing or becoming. Still having trouble? Close your eyes and explore the answer to this question: If I could do anything in the world, if I had enough money, time, and no responsibilities, what would I do?

ASSIGNMENT 12B: Write down the things you would like to accomplish no matter how small or big.

1

2

3

4

5

6

7

8

9

10

ASSIGNMENT 12C: Now you need to relax from all the "I can't" messages that have been keeping you from working toward your dreams. Look at your goals with the eyes of "I can." For your next assignment, list the steps you can take to meet your dreams. What can you do that would bring you a little closer to your big dream?

My big dream is to be a New York Times best-selling author. The first step I took toward this in the aftermath of divorce was to unpack my writing books and set up my office. It might seem small, but it got my energy and my mind focused on where I wanted to head instead of the misery of the present or the past.

How to Create the Hope that You Will Be Happy and Perhaps Even Joyful

Creating Hope 1: Healing with Time

Go to the window of your mind. Look at your thoughts, feelings, and beliefs. What do you see? What are you thinking? For even more insight, ask those who you confide in to tell you what you talk about a lot. If months and months have passed and you are still thinking a lot about your divorce, or you have constant thoughts, good or bad, about your former spouse, it still has a hold on you. There are unresolved issues that you haven't worked through yet. Remember, we are now talking about significant time passing. You first must give yourself space. Then, after the months pass, it's time to reclaim your life.

> **If the pain, anger, and frustration never seem to subside, and these thoughts are still taking up an overwhelming portion of our daily thoughts, it's time to get help.**

When we experience a hurtful event, our mind focuses on that event. This is perfectly normal human behavior. We study it as though constant analysis will provide a solution that will prevent all future hurts. The problem with this is that often we get stuck in our focus of what happened, what hurt us, how unfair it was. When we continue to dwell on the bad things in the past, we aren't living in the present. If the pain, anger, and frustration never seem to subside, and these thoughts are still taking up an overwhelming portion of our daily thoughts, it's time to get help.

If the pain, anger, and frustration never seem to subside, and these thoughts are still taking up an overwhelming portion of our daily thoughts, it's time to get help.

Creating Hope 2: Be Creative—even if it is only for 10 or 20 minutes a day.

When you sit down and start planning what you're going to do next with your life, you are being creative—you are crafting your life. Take time to identify your goals and dreams.

Now is your opportunity to paint, scrapbook, read or write poetry, goof around on the piano—whatever you used to do or have always wanted to do.

When I was going into the transition from being married to being single, I set aside time after the kids retired to bed. I needed to de-stress. I wanted to do something that I felt like doing, not writing some potential book I would sell or doing a chore in the house that needed attention. No, none of that for me.

What I did was set a date with myself. I stopped by a craft store (and I hate crafts!) on the way home from a meeting. I walked up and down the aisles, letting the child inside tell me what she wanted to do.

Although I wasn't even speaking aloud, I felt crazy. Oh well. It was time to let my inner child have a chance to tell me what she wanted. I stopped in front of a row containing coloring books and crayons. When my feet stopped, I looked at the cute coloring books on the shelves. I knew what my inner child wanted—to color. I had done that a lot when I was little, and I had forgotten how much I enjoyed it.

"Ok," I said internally. "Coloring it is."

The effects of taking a few occasions a week to color had amazing soothing results. I turned on New Age music and colored. I didn't color the way everyone says to. I broke the rules and gave the giraffe polka dots and a purple neck and was satisfied in doing so. It made me feel more alive and happy.

> **Creativity is one of the best antidotes to depression and an excellent path to healing.**

Okay, men, don't freak out. I know that coloring and doing crafts most likely isn't going to be your thing, but it is important for you to find a way to be creative. Creativity is one of the best antidotes to depression and an excellent path to healing. One newly single man decided he'd always wanted to learn how to weld. He signed up for a class. Soon he could snap the goggles over his eyes, squeeze the trigger, and as those sparks flew and the fire heated metal, his troubles seemed to melt away. He said that taking the class on welding helped him focus on something other than his divorce situation.

Creating Hope 3: Involve Yourself in the Community with Children's Activities, Religious Activities, and Social Support Groups

Becoming involved in something other than your divorce can be a great way to change the focus of your attention, get newly energized, and plug yourself into something bigger than yourself. It's important to be involved with others. When single people are by themselves too long without talking to others strange things begin to happen. They lose the grounding that contact with others can provide. There are no checks and balances left in their lives.

One of the things I did right after I was divorced was volunteer to teach children who were in abusive families. As I taught these children, my focus changed from my problems to the children and how I could help give them safeguards in situations that seemed extremely bleak. I was learning, growing, and giving. This is a great way to jumpstart the healing process.

A friend became involved in her local church. On Sundays, and for other activities, she volunteered to drive the elderly women in her area to the church house. Her life was enriched and blessed by this. The relationships she developed have continued for years. The gratitude uplifted her and she was also a great comfort to the lives she touched.

> **Becoming involved in something other than your divorce can be a great way to change the focus of your attention, get newly energized, and plug yourself into something bigger than yourself.**

Many join singles groups, parenting groups, and various other organizations offered in the community. By becoming involved, you help create a sense of belonging in your life. You are also able to serve others and do something of benefit.

There are good things you can do now in your life that you weren't able to do before, so look for opportunities and reach out to make a difference to others.

> **By becoming involved, you help create a sense of belonging in your life.**

Another single male friend enjoyed secretly doing good deeds for others. For instance, he'd noticed that the single mother in the neighborhood often forgot to take out her trash. He'd wait until dark and sneak it out to the curb for her. He shoveled snow off the walkways of ill and elderly neighbors and found many other ways to serve.

My current husband gave back to the community by becoming Mr. Fix-It Man for the elderly widows in his neighborhood. He would help out with the maintenance of their homes—small simple things like fixing a running toilet, fixing a dripping faucet, tightening a loose handle, or even changing a light bulb. None of them were huge projects. After finishing the project, he would visit, eat cookies, or join the neighbor for dinner, depending on how long he had been working. Seeing the elderly ladies excited about the help and company and lacking any pressure of future romantic involvement was extremely rewarding for him.

There are endless ways to become involved in your community. The important thing is to find something that will work for your personality and lifestyle. Your willing hand is needed, and by doing little things you can make a big difference in someone else's life.

How to Find Hope Again

1) Pay attention to how well you are healing.

2) Be creative—even if it is only for 10 or 20 minutes a day.

3) Involve yourself in the community with children's activities, religious activities, and social support groups.

Healing, like most worthwhile things, takes time and effort. Until we mourn the loss of what we no longer have, we cannot move on to a new, exciting, and enriching life. Suppressed grief will inhibit us. Another important aspect of healing that is difficult for most people is taking care of themselves. Until our basic needs are met, it is difficult to achieve anything. When we take care of ourselves, we gain the energy and strength to look honestly at the impact of our divorce. Only then will we be ready to create a new life—one where we can dream and work to make our dreams come true. When due attention is applied to our health, to mourning, and to identifying how we have been affected by our ordeal, our consciousness opens up. We become free to remember our earlier dreams and passions and return to the path of pursuing them.

> When due attention is applied to our health, to mourning, and identifying how we've been affected by this ordeal, our consciousness opens up. We become free to remember our earlier dreams and passions and get on the path to pursuing them.

To help you celebrate your accomplishments go online to www.stopmarrying mistakes.com and download **Accomplishments Celebration Form,** fill it out, and post it somewhere where you can often be reminded of your wins.

CHAPTER

3

GETTING RID
OF OLD BAGGAGE

Agood friend of mine told me she always wanted to laugh at the questionnaires at the doctor's office asking if she was married, single, or divorced. When she was divorced and single she would write to the side "free," because she didn't feel any of the offered choices fit her. She didn't like being stuck in the category of divorced. In time, she learned to accept society's title and because she later remarried, she now checks both the divorced and married boxes because both are true. Once you are divorced, that fact doesn't change. (Okay, she could go back and remarry him and maybe that would count, but she feels that would be an extreme step.) Divorce is something that never ends.

None of this means you have to carry around unnecessary baggage from your past for the rest of your life. Unresolved issues often lead to problems such as depression, self-pity, visions of revenge, wounded pride, debilitating memories, and much more. So, let's stop the cycle.

Life is full of positive and negative situations. We all have times of delight and joy, but we cannot escape every pitfall. However, when pitfalls turn into years of negative thoughts and encounters, the images, memories, and pain put us in a state of constant emotional survival. Common outcomes of extended stress are anxiety, depression, and post-traumatic stress disorder (PTSD).

(Post-traumatic stress disorder was first discovered in returning soldiers who were traumatized by their war experience. People who suffer from post-traumatic stress disorder are jumpy, have recurring dreams or flashbacks of trauma, and often feel detached or estranged from life.)

Divorce is hard, and has a way of putting us into prolonged states of stress, which cause our minds to create negative emotions and feelings that continue to plague us, sometimes years after the experiences. These are called reaction sequences. When traumatic memories crop up, many people fall into a state of stress. If we don't learn skills to deal with increased stress, we can develop ongoing and sometimes serious challenges.

> Divorce is hard, and has a way of putting us into prolonged states of stress, which cause our minds to create negative emotions and feelings that continue to plague us, sometimes yearsafter the experiences. These are called reaction sequences.

The question anyone who has been through a divorce needs to face is, "How do I get rid of these negative emotions and feelings?" I have heard many divorced people say, "I just cannot seem to get the things that my ex-spouse said or did out of my mind." Others have said, "I am so angry at my ex-spouse that I just cannot let it go." These individuals play the same memories and experiences over and over in their minds. This is what we call running mind tapes. When people mentally run these tapes, their bodies produce chemicals that flood their system. These chemicals keep them on high alert (safety mode). In other words, the mind has been signaled that something might go wrong. Those of us who constantly play tapes from the past find ourselves left with little energy. It is taxing to our bodies to be on continuous high alert. When you find yourself unable to push the pause button on your mind loop tapes, take the time to understand more about your tapes. Here's how.

Reaction Sequences

Have you ever seen someone laughing and having a good time then suddenly he or she bursts into tears? How about someone who has gone seemingly instantaneously from being mellow and happy to yelling and screaming? If you have, you may have been witnessing someone going through a reaction sequence. Sometimes people think those who act this way are crazy. It is helpful to realize what the behavior is and why the person is struggling. Perhaps then your judgments won't be so harsh. All of us have experienced a quick change of emotion at one time or another—or a reaction sequence.

> **All of us have experienced at one time or another quick change of emotion—or a reaction sequence.**

Reaction Sequence Roadmap

A reaction sequence begins with a stimulus and ends with a response. Someone experiencing a reaction sequence can shift from one emotional state to another in a short period of time. As an example, in a divorce many people develop intense negative emotions toward their spouse (or ex-spouse). Oftentimes these people begin to run the gamut of emotions, from concern to real apprehension or hatred whenever their ex is around. These feelings can be triggered by simple things such as the sound of an ex-spouse's car pulling into the driveway, hearing that particular voice on the other end of the phone, seeing his or her number on the caller ID, or a pending court date. Since contact is a common experience during the divorce proceedings, sometimes it is hard to avoid the reaction sequence.

Here's an example of how a reaction sequence could work in a divorce situation:

a. Stimulus—You see your ex-spouse's phone number on your caller ID.

b. Emotion—Instant apprehension or a wave of anger.

c. Thought—What does he/she want from me this time?

d. Chemical Release—Your body floods with adrenaline, preparing you for a pending disagreement or fight.

e. Body Language—You become tense and rigid.

d. Thought—You begin to wonder if this situation will ever end.

e. Hypothesis—I wonder if my ex-spouse will ever stop hurting me.

f. Belief—My ex-spouse is going to hurt me no matter what I do.

g. Response—I automatically become anxious and begin to panic.

Once a reaction sequence develops, it can take less than one second to go through the whole process. How does it happen so fast? Your mind remembers its experiences, both positive and negative, and it gives meaning to everything we go through. The next time something occurs that reminds us of an event and its associated meaning, our mind automatically runs the new experience through its filter—which is the related past experience. Now your mind uses this to determine how to deal with the pending situation. That is how our mind copes with negative events. Unfortunately, many negative reaction sequences are left unresolved. The result is anxiety, depression, and other negative emotions that linger, electrifying our senses even when there is no need.

Stop Marrying Mistakes

Unfortunately, many negative reaction sequences are left unresolved and the result is anxiety, depression, and other negative emotions that linger, electrifying our senses even when there is no need.

Without an understanding of how to deal with the reaction sequence, most people accelerate into constant high stress. This can cause physical health problems (e.g., headaches, ulcers, heart problems, etc.), emotional problems (e.g., depression, heightened anxiety, etc.), or both. The outcome can be debilitating or can lead people into acting out.

With so many potential side effects and ill consequences of letting the reaction run its course, it's easy to see how important it is to take the appropriate steps to deactivate your negative reaction sequences.

In order to understand the baggage you carry, take time to understand the issues that can create negative feelings and emotions. Here are a few exercises that may help you identify your own special personalized baggage.

Unfortunately, many negative reaction sequences are left unresolved and the result is anxiety, depression, and other negative emotions that linger, electrifying our senses even when there is no need.

Assignment 13

1. Evaluate the most common feelings and emotions that stem from your divorce. What are the images, memories, or events that most frequently run through your mind? Identify the issues associated with those mind tapes.

2. Review the list of the five most difficult things you have had to deal with as a result of your divorce (Chapter 1). Add to the list if more things have come up.

3. Track your emotional climate when you are thinking about your divorce. Tracking refers to following your emotions (i.e., sad, upset, angry, agitated, etc.). What triggered those emotions? Describe the pain, worry, or stress associated with those emotions.

4. Outline a reaction sequence pattern that is associated with your divorce. Continue reading to learn more about reaction sequences.

Deactivating the Reaction Sequence

Deactivating Step 1: Map It Out

The first step to deactivating a reaction sequence is to map it out. To map it out, look at the definitions and then fill out your own list below. You don't have to start at the bottom and work up or start at the top and work down. You can go in any order. If you first realize that you are experiencing a headache, then fill that spot first and work your way through the list until you complete it.

STIMULUS: What exterior event occurred to trigger an emotional/physical reaction?

EMOTION: How are you feeling as a result of the trigger?

THOUGHT: What do you think about the occurrence?

CHEMICAL RELEASE: This is an involuntary physical reaction of your body as a reaction to the triggers.

BODY LANGUAGE: How are you holding your body? Neck forward? Shoulders slouched? Is your stomach hurting?

THOUGHT: What additional thoughts are you having?

HYPOTHESIS: What do you believe this event or action might mean about yourself, others, and life.

BELIEF: What do you believe as a result of this, or which belief is reconfirmed?

RESPONSE: What is your reaction to the trigger.

Your turn.

STIMULUS:

EMOTION:

THOUGHT:

CHEMICAL RELEASE:

BODY LANGUAGE:

THOUGHT:

HYPOTHESIS:

BELIEF:

RESPONSE:

The next time the reaction sequence runs through your mind, you'll be able to realize what's happening.

Deactivating Step 2: The Name

Some people find it useful to give the reaction sequence a name. The reason for this is when a reaction sequence occurs and there is a way to identify the particular reaction, the person who named the reaction sequence is more likely to figure out what is happening to them and stop it from continuing.

For example, one woman labeled her negative mind tape, "The Train." She said that when the negative thoughts began they built up steam until they moved "full steam ahead." At that point, she realized the reaction sequence had gotten the best of her.

Deactivating Step 3: Evaluate the Impact

After you have identified your reaction sequence step-by-step and named it, the next step is to evaluate how the reaction sequence has impacted you. This might sound easier than it is. Let's look at the reaction sequence example of seeing your former spouse's name on the caller ID. How often did the byproduct of you being anxious, angry, or sure he/she is just messing with you affect your conversation? How many phone calls could have gone differently and not ended up in another fight? How often did your increased stress lead you to become snappy with the kids or not being completely tuned into their needs because you were struggling to deal with your nerves? Did this affect your sleep? Your health? Your relationships with others? Did it increase problems with your former spouse?

As you can tell from the list of questions, people who have full-blown reaction sequences suffer as a result and affect others around them. Think about your reactions and be honest about what it is costing you and those with whom you are sharing relationships.

Deactivating Step 4: A Game Plan

Once you have completed these steps, you will need to create a new planned response for when the reaction sequence begins in the future. This is what we call a game plan. Your game plan should include a clear step-by-step approach of what you will run in your mind whenever the reaction sequence begins. The more specific you are with the game plan, the more successful you'll be in having a different response the next time the stimulus occurs.

EXAMPLE: The next time I see that my former spouse's name is on the caller ID, I am going to take a deep breath and check in with myself. Is my heart beating faster? Is my stomach knotting? Are my shoulders tightening?

If my heart is beating fast, I will take three, slow, deep breaths. If my stomach is knotting, I will focus on relaxing my stomach muscles. If my shoulders are tensing, I will focus on loosening them. If I then feel more at ease, I will check inside and see if I can talk to my former spouse from a calm place. If I can, great, I will answer the phone, reminding myself that I don't have to say yes and I can take my time in answering any requests.

If I don't think I can stay grounded and focused, then I won't answer the phone. When I feel ready, I will check my phone messages and see what was wanted. This way I will not react.

If I still don't think I can calm down when my former spouse calls me, I will ask that all further communication be by email. Also, I will remind myself that getting worked up and suffering all the things that I wrote down in the impact section isn't worth it. I won't give my former spouse that satisfaction, and I don't want to do this to me.

Hey, not wanting to give my former spouse any more power to hurt me has stopped more than one reaction sequence. It really motivates me to stop the adrenaline from flowing. Maybe it will work the same magic for you.

NOTE: Like almost everything else, stopping reaction sequences will not happen automatically. The more practice you give it, the better you'll become. If you pay attention to what is happening to you, the better you will be at getting control over your triggers.

I felt stupid when I first learned this concept and then realized that a reaction sequence had again run its full course before I became aware of what was happening. More likely than not, at first you will become aware of a reaction sequence happening without your knowing it at the time. When you become alert to this happening, you are two thirds of the way to solving the problem. By really paying attention, you'll start recognizing patterns that get you in trouble. This is great because then you can put the game plan into action. You're programming your brain to become sensitive to reaction sequences.

I realized I was suffering from a reaction sequence when my former spouse called and wanted something. I would always automatically say, "No." I had the belief that my ex always took advantage of me and I needed to stand up for myself. Although the belief had truth, it did not best serve me. I realized that if I stopped and thought about what my ex was asking for, and it was reasonable, it wouldn't hurt me to say, "Yes," sometimes. This would improve our relationship and make it more likely to get a yes out of him if I ever needed a favor. The game plan I came up with was this: every time my former spouse called and wanted something, no matter what it was, I would tell him that I would think about it and get back to him. This allowed me space to contemplate what he wanted and how I really felt about the situation. It also granted me time if I needed to bounce the request off someone else to help me decide if what he asked was unreasonable and pushing the boundaries or if it was a reasonable request. It also gave me room to consider how my response might affect the future.

This technique has worked extremely well. We don't fight as often on the phone. I feel more in control and not so pressured into doing something I might regret. All in all, it creates for me the space I need to make more informed decisions.

With this game plan properly in place, I can see his number on my phone and no longer react. Instead of dreading the conversation, I feel confident that I can handle whatever the subject is because I know that I will not commit until I am ready.

Steps to Deactivate A Reaction Sequence

STEP ONE: Map It Out

STEP TWO: Name It

STEP THREE: Evaluate the Impact

STEP FOUR: Game Plan

Now it's your turn.

ASSIGNMENT 14A: Take time to identify one of your reaction sequences. Start with the stimulus or what triggers your thoughts and feelings and end with how you respond.

a. Stimulus

b. Emotion

c. Thought

d. Chemical release

e. Body language

f. Thought

g. Hypothesis

h. Belief

i. Response/Behavior

It's important to understand the significant impact that your reaction sequences have upon your life. They affect your thoughts, emotions, and behaviors. One of my colleagues once said, "I am the sum of my reaction sequences." Her point was that she had become so accustomed to the patterns in her life that seldom did she have experiences that appeared new to her.

Here is another example of how someone else described the impact of her reaction sequence, "Every time I start thinking about my ex-spouse I get nauseous," she told me. "Sometimes it takes hours to get my stomach back to normal." If she didn't get this side-effect under control she could be heading for serious health conditions. You might be on the same path as her. It's time to explore what is happening.

Go to www.stopmarryingmistakes.com to download your **Reaction Sequences Worksheet.** Work through the process as many times as needed until you achieve a state of peace.

ASSIGNMENT 14B: How has the reaction sequence you described in the previous assignment impacted you? How has it affected the relationships around you? Has it affected your work? Has the reaction sequence influenced other areas in your life?

When you understand your reaction sequences and how they impact your emotional and physical health, it's time to create a plan that will enable you to stop and evaluate the reaction sequence so that you are in charge of it rather than it being in charge of you. You cannot be in charge of it if you are constantly running mind tapes like those described above.

ASSIGNMENT 14C: Develop a game plan for the reaction sequence you outlined in 14a. Your game plan should include specific thoughts or actions you will take once the reaction sequence begins.

EXAMPLE: The next time I begin running the "Blaming Game" tape, I am going to take time and write down what I am feeling and thinking. If I don't have time to write, I am going to make a list of five positive things in my life, which is another way to stop the reaction sequences.

How to Take Responsibility for Your Actions and Move On

During a divorce, many feel compelled to explain to others why the relationship is ending. If children are involved, they are informed that Mom and Dad are divorcing. Others given the news are family members, attorneys, clergymen, coworkers, and friends. With the onslaught of questions about why, the situation can become painful, uncomfortable, and embarrassing.

More often than not, the divorcing couple tells completely different stories about why their marriage is ending. This can create high conflict, especially when one or both attempt to make their ex-spouse look bad.

I have spoken with a therapist who has met with many couples near the end of their marriages. It's interesting how the issues presented in therapy get blown out of proportion when there is a custody battle, when division of assets are being discussed, or when one decides to remarry. Most people are stunned when they hear the stories their ex-spouse tells about them. This often leads to a lot of pain and confusion. They wonder why their ex cannot let go. Why do they feel compelled to share their ugliness with everyone?

I have also observed that people who heal the quickest seldom feel the need to paint the worst picture of their ex-spouse. If the focus is constantly on the former spouse and how horrible they are, the negative energy a person creates will return time and time again. In fact, those who are willing to openly explore their own misbehaviors and acknowledge what they did to contribute to the divorce heal much faster.

Those who are willing to openly explore their own misbehaviors and acknowledge what they did to contribute to the divorce heal much faster.

Those who acknowledge their faults open the path for personal growth and development. If you are willing to identify what you did wrong, and what you could have done better, you will be prepared to move on. There is one big challenge in these assignments: it is hard to know if you actually did the things your ex-partner says you did or if you're accepting too much of the blame. Your personal growth in completing this assignment will depend on how honest you are with yourself. Honesty, in this instance, requires that you take responsibility for your misconduct and no more.

Please be aware that if you take more or less responsibility than you should, you may be hurting yourself.

Take a few minutes now to assess your role and contributions to the marriage. Be honest with yourself and only take into consideration your misconduct. Remember: take the appropriate responsibility for what happened.

ASSIGNMENT 15A: Make a list of things you did during your marriage that contributed to the problems. This is not a fun list to create, but it can be educational and healing if you are willing to honestly examine your behaviors. If you don't take the time to look at your part and responsibilities and you do enter another relationship, you'll make the same mistakes and head toward the same results. People repeat their problems until they acknowledge them. Once they are aware of them, they may be successful at moving past them.

1

2

3

4

5

6

7

8

9

10

ASSIGNMENT 15B: Write a letter addressed to your ex-spouse in which you take responsibility for the things you did to contribute to the problems in your marriage. Please note: This letter is for your benefit and does not need to be sent. If you choose to send it, it could be therapeutic for you and your ex-spouse, or it could be something that is used against you. You will have to judge based upon your own instincts and knowledge of your ex-spouse whether sending it to him or her is appropriate for you. In the space provided below, write the key points that you would cover in your letter.

1

2

3

4

5

6

7

8

9

10

ASSIGNMENT 15C: Now that you've identified things that you could have done better, which of these things would you like to change the most? Write down the things you can do now to create those changes.

1

2

3

4

5

6

7

8

9

10

Getting rid of baggage can be extremely painful at first. Once you get into it and start feeling better, the shedding of past junk can be freeing. The key to not letting your past rule you is to understand your reaction sequences, take the necessary steps to conquer them, and move forward to build the life you want.

HOW TO STOP DEPRESSION BEFORE IT SINKS TOO DEEPLY

Depression is a common problem for those going through a divorce. I have seen some of the most dynamic and outgoing people fall into real slumps during and after a divorce. Learning to stop depression before it sinks in too deeply requires a clear understanding of what is triggering it. Is it loss, loneliness, broken dreams, fears of the unknown, heightened financial burdens, lack of social support, a combination of all of these things, or something else?

On the next page you'll find a model that describes depression. As you look at this model, you'll see a boy on the right whose self-worth is intact. On the lower right hand part you will see a picture of the same boy who feels like he is of no value to anyone. Sometimes we already have depression from escalating problems our marriage was encountering or from other past issues.

The task at hand is to learn how to stand tall again with your self-worth intact. This can be accomplished as you identify how your divorce and/or marriage impacted your own self-worth. Take some time to review this model. You will see choice point number one. At this stage, a person chooses to accept or reject the barrage of invalidation they are receiving. There is no question that divorce includes a significant amount of negative feedback. At choice point number two, a person determines how they are going to respond to the negative feedback or barrage of invalidation. The assignments below will help you evaluate where you are in this depression model.

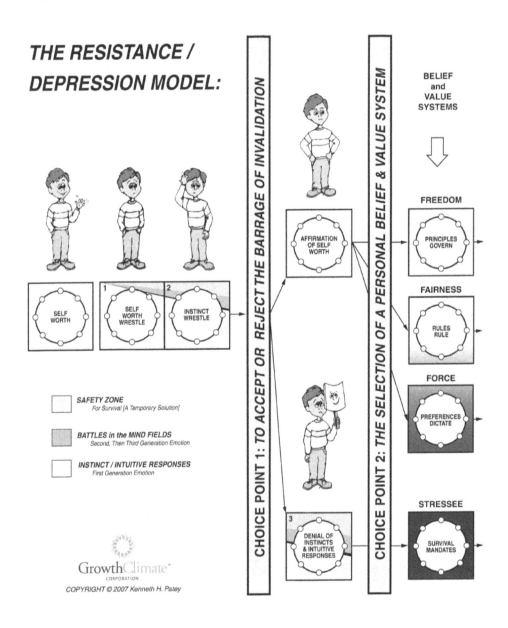

THE RESISTANCE / DEPRESSION MODEL:

CHOICE POINT 1: TO ACCEPT OR REJECT THE BARRAGE OF INVALIDATION

CHOICE POINT 2: THE SELECTION OF A PERSONAL BELIEF & VALUE SYSTEM

BELIEF and VALUE SYSTEMS

SELF WORTH

1 SELF WORTH WRESTLE

2 INSTINCT WRESTLE

AFFIRMATION OF SELF WORTH

3 DENIAL OF INSTINCTS & INTUITIVE RESPONSES

FREEDOM — PRINCIPLES GOVERN

FAIRNESS — RULES RULE

FORCE — PREFERENCES DICTATE

STRESSEE — SURVIVAL MANDATES

SAFETY ZONE
For Survival! [A Temporary Solution]

BATTLES in the MIND FIELDS
Second, Then Third Generation Emotion

INSTINCT / INTUITIVE RESPONSES
First Generation Emotion

GrowthClimate
CORPORATION

COPYRIGHT © 2007 Kenneth H. Patey

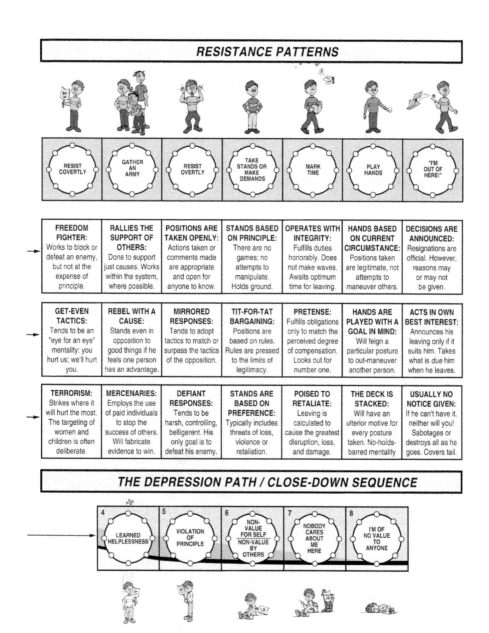

RESISTANCE PATTERNS

FREEDOM FIGHTER:	RALLIES THE SUPPORT OF OTHERS:	POSITIONS ARE TAKEN OPENLY:	STANDS BASED ON PRINCIPLE:	OPERATES WITH INTEGRITY:	HANDS BASED ON CURRENT CIRCUMSTANCE:	DECISIONS ARE ANNOUNCED:
Works to block or defeat an enemy, but not at the expense of principle.	Done to support just causes. Works within the system, where possible.	Actions taken or comments made are appropriate and open for anyone to know.	There are no games; no attempts to manipulate. Holds ground.	Fulfills duties honorably. Does not make waves. Awaits optimum time for leaving.	Positions taken are legitimate, not attempts to maneuver others.	Resignations are official. However, reasons may or may not be given.
GET-EVEN TACTICS:	**REBEL WITH A CAUSE:**	**MIRRORED RESPONSES:**	**TIT-FOR-TAT BARGAINING:**	**PRETENSE:**	**HANDS ARE PLAYED WITH A GOAL IN MIND:**	**ACTS IN OWN BEST INTEREST:**
Tends to be an "eye for an eye" mentality: you hurt us; we'll hurt you.	Stands even in opposition to good things if he feels one person has an advantage.	Tends to adopt tactics to match or surpass the tactics of the opposition.	Positions are based on rules. Rules are pressed to the limits of legitimacy.	Fulfills obligations only to match the perceived degree of compensation. Looks out for number one.	Will feign a particular posture to out-maneuver another person.	Announces his leaving only if it suits him. Takes what is *due* him when he leaves.
TERRORISM:	**MERCENARIES:**	**DEFIANT RESPONSES:**	**STANDS ARE BASED ON PREFERENCE:**	**POISED TO RETALIATE:**	**THE DECK IS STACKED:**	**USUALLY NO NOTICE GIVEN:**
Strikes where it will hurt the most. The targeting of women and children is often deliberate.	Employs the use of paid individuals to stop the success of others. Will fabricate evidence to win.	Tends to be harsh, controlling, belligerent. His only goal is to defeat his enemy.	Typically includes threats of loss, violence or retaliation.	Leaving is calculated to cause the greatest disruption, loss, and damage.	Will have an ulterior motive for every posture taken. No-holds-barred mentality	If he can't have it, neither will you! Sabotages or destroys all as he goes. Covers tail.

THE DEPRESSION PATH / CLOSE-DOWN SEQUENCE

Understanding the Levels of Depression

It's vital to understand how depression pulls you down into a pit before you can climb out. We're talking here, of course, about depression that stems from an event like divorce and not clinical depression. This second type of depression requires the help of doctors and sometimes drug therapy. If the problem with depression continues for you and doesn't seem to subside after your divorce, seek professional help.

We are going to discuss in further depth how a person reaches depression then show you how to take steps back out.

Depression Step 1: Self-Worth

Most people are born with self-worth. How often have you heard a baby complain about his nose being too big or her skin having too many baby pimples? It just doesn't happen. What happens when you tell a typical two-year-old girl that she looks cute in her new dress? Most often the girl will beam and twirl around in a circle to show off the ruffles. The two-year-old girl knows at that moment she's beautiful. She has no doubt. Most two-year-olds also know that they are loved or feel they are. That is not something they usually worry about. So what happens to us and this great feeling of magnificence?

Life. People. Some people deliberately hurt the self-esteem of others. The majority of people don't intentionally try to hurt someone else, but adults do sometimes say things that can cause a child to begin to question his or her own worth. Some questions might be:

- Who do you think you are?

- Why did you do that? Don't you know that it is better to do it this way?

- Don't you know anything?

Or people make statements that have an eroding effect.

- Man, you can't do anything right.

- You did that wrong.

- I can't believe how thoughtless you are.

Besides negative comments or repeated put-downs, we begin to struggle if we endure ridicule or negative reactions to our decisions, ideas, and feelings. Exposure to this type of treatment can be found everywhere. When confronted by this type of behavior, it is natural to have an immediate resistance. Think back to the first time your spouse put you down. If you can recall that memory, it was more than likely painful for you.

For me, it happened on our wedding day. We had just gone through the ceremony and had joined arms to pose for the photographer. I beamed. I had married my Prince Charming and my life was now going to be perfect. As we smiled and posed for the camera something negative slipped out of my husband's mouth. I don't remember what he said, but I do remember sucking in my breath and feeling surprise and a jabbing hurt. I let it pass. Surely he didn't mean it. His words were a mistake or I misunderstood.

It wasn't until after the reception when we were climbing into our car that another attack occurred. I am hypoglycemic, and standing in line to greet people for hours had taken a toll on me. My blood sugar had dropped, which meant my stomach had tightened, I was lightheaded, and dizzy. I said, "Oh, I don't feel well."

A long discourse about how I was ruining his wedding spilled from his mouth. At this point I did what is natural for people to do when being attacked. I resisted. Some people protest by outwardly fighting back. Others keep it inside, burying it underneath a myriad of emotion. At that point, because I wasn't used to him attacking my worth, I reacted by outwardly fighting back. When I rejected his message my self-worth stayed intact. It wasn't until later, when I started believing his messages that something must be wrong with me, that I stepped onto the path of depression.

Depression Step 2: Instinct Wrestle

Sometimes the self-worth wrestle can stem from more subtle statements, such as when you ask a child to stop crying. If a person who is a significant figure in their life tells them, "There's nothing to cry about. Stop your bawling," children will more than likely start wondering what is wrong with them. Their feelings told them they were upset, and now someone they respect and trust tells them they are upset over nothing. If children at that moment believe the authority figure is right and their instincts and beliefs are wrong, they have graduated into the "Instinct Wrestle" part of the journey.

Adults can also take an instinct wrestle trip. I bought my ticket about three years into my marriage when my parents called and informed me that after twenty-six years of marriage they were getting a divorce. The news hit me like a mountain falling on my head. I asked them why, heard my mother's weak voice pleading for understanding, and heard my parents' reassurance that the divorce would be amicable. I remember fighting a tremendous urge to hang up the phone and flee. When I did get off the phone, I huddled in the corner of my kitchen against the cabinets. I curled up into the fetal position, tears streaming down my face as huge sobs erupted. My perfect family dream was over. I did not know that the divorce of one's parents could be so painful.

My husband heard the noise and came to find out what was wrong. As he listened to the news he said, "Get over it. It's no big deal. You knew that they were going to eventually get divorced. They didn't get along very well anyway."

Through the next few days and months this message was repeated many times. I fought him on his words. A person's parents getting divorced was a big deal. My family, as I knew it, was ending. I might never have my family back together in one place. (Over ten years later, I still haven't.) I saw it as the destruction of my family.

My husband's repeated insistence that I was "making a big deal over nothing," affected my thoughts and beliefs. My beliefs and decisions on how to grieve over my parents' divorce had been challenged. When your reactions, decisions, beliefs, or feelings are called into question, you enter into a self-worth challenge.

When my husband questioned my feelings, I wondered if I was creating a bigger problem than necessary. What was wrong with me? I felt all this pain and hurt and wanted to cry. Why couldn't I just put it aside and go on with life? As the divorce proceedings continued, and the ugliness and division of who was talking to who started, I felt less and expressed less until months later when I heard our family's theme song. Then I was suddenly in tears. I was shocked and couldn't understand why I was having such a dramatic reaction. I didn't understand then that I was denying my feelings. At this stage I questioned and doubted my internal guidance system, which is a dangerous position. It makes us more vulnerable and threatens our sense of well-being, our sense of a secure place in the world. When a person denies his or her feelings it comes out in strange ways. My husband's pain and hurt came out through his fists. I experienced some emotional outbursts, but mostly I was in a state of non-feeling.

Depression Step 3: Choice Point 1

If we exist in the turmoil between believing what our internal instincts are telling us and believing the opposite message our significant other is saying, we enter a crossroads, which Growth Climate has labeled Choice Point 1. We must choose whether to accept the doubts that are beginning to form or reject them and continue to value what we sense has worth within ourselves.

When I came to this choice point I thought about my husband and his love for me. He would only tell me these things about myself because he cared. What was wrong with me? Why couldn't I just go on like other people in my family seemed to be able to do? As the thoughts continued, I chose the next step of believing that I lacked worth. If I had reflected on the people who did show me I had value, or if I would have looked at other things my husband said that validated my worth, my self-concept would have remained intact. Instead, I believed those things he told me I lacked.

Depression Step 4: Choice Point 2

When I accepted the message that something was wrong with me and that I shouldn't be having negative feelings about what was happening to my family, I formed a belief and value system that would keep my new thoughts and beliefs in place. Obviously those beliefs that I wasn't of value put me in danger. In those early years, before I got treatment and started to reclaim my life, I never thought about leaving my situation because I had beliefs that kept me there. Although I hated being scared and hurting from my husband's physical abuse, I thought something was wrong with me and that when I fixed it my husband would stop hurting me. I took all the responsibility of our difficulties onto my shoulders.

Ironically, my husband, who told me it was no big deal when parents divorced, flipped out royally when his parents decided to divorce six months after mine. This taught me a lesson. Often people impose on us what they themselves wouldn't believe if they experienced it. If I had understood that my husband's words and actions were a direct result of his problems, I wouldn't have accepted his comments about my pain.

You may not have formed the same beliefs as I did, but think back to the negative messages your former spouse or other significant people in your life sent you or that you interpreted as negative. Think about how they affected you and your relationship. See how your beliefs led you to depression and/or being less of the person you really are.

In a marriage that has ended in divorce, there have to be places or events where each person comes up to Choice Point 1 and must determine what to do with the negativity that is being presented. Take a look at what happened for you. Answer the questions below. It is important to do the writing and think about, in detail, what happened with you. If you can see the road map that got you into depression, then you will figure out the guideposts to get back out.

To assist you with understanding and mastering the steps of depression in the different personality styles go to www.stopmarryingmistakes.com and download the **Steps of Depression Flash Cards**.

For me, I had to start believing in my internal guidance system again. I needed to learn how to trust that my feelings were okay.

We will go into deeper detail about the ways to climb out of depression later. First do the exercises and get a baseline of where you are.

Assignment 16a: Review the boxes that begin with "self-worth" and end with "I'm of no value to anyone." Where would you place yourself? Why? Where would you place yourself in the most difficult part of your marriage? What was the most difficult part of your divorce?

Do you remember the first time your worth was challenged in your marriage? How did you handle it? Were there times when you started believing the negative messages sent to you? What did you believe? How did it affect you?

ASSIGNMENT 16B: Outline how your feelings of depression have changed throughout your divorce. When have you noticed a change in your mood? What has created the change for good or bad?

ASSIGNMENT 16C: In order to understand depression, you must understand the climate around you. If you are a person who became depressed during your divorce, write down a list of things around you that contributed to your depression. If you were depressed before your divorce, try to recall all the things that you believe have contributed to it. Remember that many times depression comes from being in a situation where we feel we can't be true to ourselves, or when we listen to negative feedback and start to believe that we lack worth or value.

ASSIGNMENT 16D: If you were depressed but are no longer feeling depressed, what pulled you out of your depression? What can you do to safeguard yourself so you won't fall into depression again? What are the signs that let you know that you might be heading for depression? Are there people that you can talk to about this? Ask them to be supportive and gently point out when you might be heading toward depression again.

There are many things that you can do to stop depression before it sinks in too deeply. Below you will find a list of ideas that may help you stop your depression.

If you are depressed, these things can also be very helpful in assisting you with climbing back out.

a) Exercise 3–5 times a week.

b) Get involved in activities with other singles.

c) Eat healthy food.

d) Make a list of things that you would like to accomplish.

e) Read a good, uplifting book.

f) Write down your inner thoughts and feelings.

g) Identify the climate or environment that triggers your depression and try to be in that climate less often.

h) Monitor your energy level. When it is low, do things that will increase your energy.

i) When negative thoughts start playing in your mind, recognize them and give yourself permission to turn off the tape.

j) Affirm your value through meditation. Write a list of things that are great about you and spend some time remembering who you really are.

Getting rid of your past baggage is one of the best ways to counter depression. To succeed in addressing past issues and moving on requires you to figure out where you are on the depression scale, then start working yourself back to the more authentic, happier you. You can do this work. It's a vital step in the journey toward finding joy after divorce.

CHAPTER

5

BELIEVING IN YOURSELF

If you have been divorced one or more times, learning to have faith in yourself and your ability to have successful relationships is critical to your future success with others. This chapter will help you believe in yourself. You will come to see the power of your beliefs as they relate to your sense of self and your relationships.

During our lives, we create beliefs in our own minds about who we are and who we are not. We hear statements about how people view themselves such as, "I am shy," or "I am not very good at relationships," or "I am not very much fun to be with," or "Nobody would want me, I'm too old." These are common pronouncements of what people are thinking. Each of us has a perception of self that directly impacts how we interact with people. Whether we are confident or shy, scared of relationships or excited about them, is largely dependent upon the beliefs we have about ourselves and people in general. While our identity is formed at an early age, it continues to change and develop over the years based upon our experiences. Our self-concept is impacted significantly by our parents, teachers, leaders, peers, and, eventually, by those with whom we seek close and intimate relationships. Sadly, many of us have experienced significant pain and hurt in our lives, thus causing us to stop believing in ourselves.

A therapist friend had a woman come in to see him who disclosed many significant hardships she had experienced throughout her childhood, including abuse. She tried to ignore and hide the fact that she had been sexually abused. At the time, she did not think anyone would believe her. She thought she would be punished. Consequently, she carried that burden with her. She did not feel close to anyone, not even her parents. When her parents divorced this distanced her further. She felt isolated and alone.

> **Sadly, many of us have experienced significant pain and hurt in our lives, thus causing us to stop believing in ourselves.**

Throughout their discussion I had a sense that she had never had the opportunity to connect with another human being. She verbalized her belief that "no one wants me." This was one of the many negative beliefs that she had formed about herself because of her childhood experiences. Her beliefs were deeply ingrained in how she saw herself and others. She believed she was flawed and that she would never succeed in any relationship.

Such powerful, long-standing beliefs are not easy to overcome. As an adult, her challenge has been to learn how to value herself. Like many people, she wants to experience a positive connection with others. However, the risk involved in meeting and reaching out to new people has been daunting. She lacks the tools to even know how to start forming connections. She has to learn and relearn some of the most important lessons in life: that she is of infinite worth, that she has much to offer, and that she can succeed in relationships. Those lessons require risk and high self-awareness.

All of us have formed conclusions about our own worth. In this chapter you will be asked to identify some of the beliefs you have about yourself. As you gain insight, you will understand more fully why you do what you do. However, before you begin identifying your personal beliefs, it may be helpful to understand more about the human mind and how it develops these convictions.

The Human Mind

Ninety-five percent of what we know about the capabilities of the human brain has been learned in the last twenty years (Gelb, 1998). This understanding has helped us gain better insights about how we function and what processes we go through during stressful events. We have discovered how our minds react when in crisis or prolonged stress. Additionally, we have learned how brain chemistry can actually be altered by constant pressure and stress.

Many mental health disorders can be linked to what is occurring inside our minds. Therefore, if we want to understand ourselves better, we must decipher how the mind works. The chart on the next page will help you identify how the stage is set in creating beliefs about ourselves.

As you look at this chart, you will see the sensory input on the left hand side. Even before we are born, our senses are turned on. Unborn children do have the ability to respond to input.

I was surprised to discover how much an unborn child responds to outside events. When I was five months pregnant with my first child she started to kick, which is normal. What I noticed was that when my husband walked into the room and talked, she immediately kicked and punched. We tried experimenting and discovered that this child became excited at the sound of his voice. When my oldest was born she often had colic. I would hand her to her dad so he could talk to her and calm her. She would nestle into his chest and stop crying. This is how I became convinced that my oldest child is a daddy's girl. She has always been and always will be. (Belief.)

Here's another example of unborn children developing sensory receptors. When I was pregnant with my sixth child, I enrolled the other children in swimming lessons. I was in a Mother and Tot class with the youngest. Every time I climbed into the cold water, *boom*, the unborn child's foot jabbed my side. For two weeks, every day, I climbed into the pool and my unborn child jabbed his foot into me.

Most women who have had a baby have stories like this. What does this mean in relationship to how the mind works?

Once the five key senses start functioning, the human mind begins to gather information. At an early age, the mind collects data, allowing it to succeed in its environment, good or bad. Inside your brain there is an area called the reticular formation. The reticular formation determines what information your brain will pay attention to and what information it will push aside.

Why is there a filtering system?

The mind receives approximately 100,000,000 pieces of input every second. Brain overload would definitely occur without a filtering system in place.

For example, when my youngest son was a toddler he was diagnosed with sensory overload disorder. This meant he had a hard time filtering the sensory information. If he got the smallest amount of water on his clothes he would cry until his shirt was changed. He would scream frantically if his bare skin touched grass. He couldn't stand how it felt. By the time I sought treatment, he would cry for hours if I put shoes on his feet. He complained they hurt. With the treatment I sought and doing some sensory integration exercises at home, my son was able to overcome his disorder. Being overly sensitive to the incoming sensory data can drive a person literally crazy, so the job of the reticular formation is crucial. We need this filter in order to maintain sanity.

The important thing to know about the reticular formation is that it does take in all the information and makes a record of it. Thus, all the data is stored in our memory banks.

Another job the reticular formation performs is paying attention to and sending out alerts if it discovers an event that is of value, threatening, unusual, or special. The reticular formation will send out a warning to your conscious mind to interpret the event and determine how threatening the new information is. If the information is *not* of value, threatening, unusual, or special, it goes directly to your memory banks and bypasses the conscious mind.

Let's combine how the human mind works with the beliefs that we have acquired. Imagine that you are involved in a dating relationship. The relationship begins with many fun and exciting dates. You begin forming an idea of the character of the person you're dating. During the early phases, you're paying close attention to behaviors and emotions. You determine that he/she is kind, patient, and considerate. You don't see many things that bother you. You begin to get motivated about the potential possibilities of this relationship. Your mind has been gathering a lot of positive data with very few negative pieces of information. Things are looking good or at least you think so.

After dating six to eight weeks, the person you are dating calls to tell you that he/she has had a bad day at work. You try to offer help but don't know what to say. You hear a bit of sarcasm and frustration during the phone conversation, but you don't think much of it because it seems like the normal response a person would have in this situation. Later that evening, when the two of you get together, you sense something has changed. You cannot put your finger on it, but something is strange. You feel like you have to be more careful about what you say and do. You notice that he/she is uptight, edgy, and curt. You ask, "What's wrong?" The response you get surprises you. He/she begins to complain about everything, including his/her relationship with you. You're not accustomed to this, so you start defending yourself. This causes him/her to suggest that maybe you shouldn't see each other anymore.

ASSIGNMENT 17A: Given this case scenario, how would you respond?

ASSIGNMENT 17B: Write down the thoughts you would have about this person.

ASSIGNMENT 17C: What are some of the feelings you would have about yourself?

Identify your thoughts and inner emotions.

Notice how your mind processes the event. Is the situation of value, threatening, unusual? Absolutely. Because the experience you just had with this person is unique or a threat (part of your alert list), your mind must determine what to do. It attempts to make sense of the entire unusual happening. The information goes straight to the conscious mind and you work on attaching meaning to the situation.

If this reminds you of a previous experience, you may quickly decide that this relationship is just like your other relationships. Your mind does not have to take much time processing that this person is a jerk. However, if you have never had anything like this happen before, your mind may struggle to give it meaning. It may take hours, days, or weeks to come to a conclusion. You may ask advice from friends or you may get a phone call from your date apologizing for his/her behavior. This is new information, and you will have to once again give meaning to what is happening. You may find yourself asking, "Is he or she being real?" or "Can I trust him/her?" At some point you have to make a judgment. How you judge this experience will establish what happens in this relationship. It will also determine what conclusions you make about this person and yourself.

Let's say that you decide to get back together. You have convinced yourself that he or she will not act like that again, or that he or she was just having a bad day. Now suppose that a few weeks later something similar occurs. You conclude that this is not a fluke but a character trait of the person you're dating. You end the relationship, believing you cannot trust him or her.

If you had experienced other relationships similar to this one, it would not be too farfetched to assume that *all* men or women will hurt you. This could be your belief. The outcome could be that you will be more guarded, consciously and unconsciously, in subsequent dating relationships. This is how our minds create beliefs which, in turn, impact our behaviors.

Self-Judgment

Another interesting element that stems from our relationships with others is that we have the opportunity to make judgments of our own conduct. Whether we want to or not, we tend to make judgments about ourselves. This is how we form beliefs about self—sadly, many people form negative beliefs. This happens most frequently when we receive negative information about ourselves, or when we perceive that we have failed at something.

> **Whether we want to or not, we tend to make judgments about ourselves.**

When relationships go bad, many people assume that they have failed. This is especially true of people who have gone through a lot of relationships. They ask themselves, "What's wrong with me?" or "Why do I attract people who will hurt me?" or "Why do I always fail in relationships?" Such questions are significant and should not be dismissed. Each of these statements is a belief. If people honestly believe that there is something wrong with themselves or that they always fail in relationships, they will act consistently with their beliefs. They may even sabotage their relationships because of their beliefs.

> **If people honestly believe that there is something wrong with themselves or that they always fail in relationships, they will act consistently with their beliefs.**

A therapist friend is familiar with a case where a woman was really starting to like her boyfriend, but she felt like she had to hold back until she knew that he would not hurt her. As a result, she was emotionally reserved. Her boyfriend picked up on her feelings and tried to comfort her. He attempted to get her to open up and be close to him, but she refused. Eventually, he quit trying. As she evaluated this experience, she realized that she had operated under a deep-seated belief that she was not lovable. Her unresolved issues caused her to hide her deepest emotions, which in turn led to the end of that relationship.

Clearly, when our mind believes there is something wrong with us, we have internalized a negative belief about our self. Once a belief is in place, our mind stops looking for more information to confirm or deny it. Consequently, assumptions are made without evaluating whether the belief is true or not. In the story above, this woman's belief was that she was unlovable. Had she taken the time to evaluate why she was withholding love and care from her boyfriend, she may have realized that he was loving her. She couldn't see clearly through the constant replay of her mind tapes telling her she was unlovable. Her own faulty conclusions prevented her from developing a relationship with someone who legitimately tried to connect with her.

Finding the "Real" You

During and after a divorce you're forced to give meaning to why it happened. You might try to figure out what went wrong and why and what you're going to do about it. In the midst of all of these questions, you may ask, "What did I do to make this person stop loving me?" or "Am I that bad, that he or she would not want me?" or "Why was I so stupid to marry a jerk like that?" At the root of these questions is the pain and hurt that carries over from the beliefs you've formed about yourself.

If you want to speed up the healing process, you must first identify the beliefs you have about yourself. Do you think you're worthy and valuable, or do you think that something about you is flawed? Remember, a person can have a whole host of beliefs. For instance, you might believe in yourself and your abilities as a parent or in your career but at the same time believe that you're a failure in the area of intimate relationships. We often globalize beliefs such as "I am a failure," when the true belief you have is that you are a specific failure when it comes to personal relationships or being independent.

Below is another assignment that will aid you in determining your own beliefs and where you are getting stuck.

If you want to speed up the healing process, you must first identify the beliefs you have about yourself.

ASSIGNMENT 18A: On a scale of one to ten, with ten being "I am confident and believe I am a good person," how would you score yourself? (Circle the answer that most correctly represents how you feel about yourself).

1   2   3   4   5   6   7   8   9   10

ASSIGNMENT 18B: Explain your answer.

Now we are going to break down your beliefs into nine different areas of your life. We want to pinpoint the areas that need attention in order for you to feel better about yourself.

1–On a scale of one to ten, with ten being "I am confident and believe I am a good employee/employer," how would you score yourself? (Circle the answer that most correctly represents how you feel about yourself).

1   2   3   4   5   6   7   8   9   10

ASSIGNMENT 18C: Explain your answer.

2–On a scale of one to ten, with ten being "I am confident and believe I am a good parent/son/daughter," how would you score yourself? (Circle the answer that most correctly represents how you feel about yourself).

1   2   3   4   5   6   7   8   9   10

ASSIGNMENT 18D: Explain your answer.

3–On a scale of one to ten, with ten being "I am confident and believe I am a spiritual person," how would you score yourself? (Circle the answer that most correctly represents how you feel about yourself).

1   2   3   4   5   6   7   8   9   10

ASSIGNMENT 18E: Explain your answer.

4–On a scale of one to ten, with ten being "I am confident and believe I am good at providing for myself and/or my family," how would you score yourself? (Circle the answer that most correctly represents how you feel about yourself).

1   2   3   4   5   6   7   8   9   10

ASSIGNMENT 18F: Explain your answer.

5–On a scale of one to ten, with ten being "I am confident and believe I am good at taking care of my health," how would you score yourself? (Circle the answer that most correctly represents how you feel about yourself).

1   2   3   4   5   6   7   8   9   10

ASSIGNMENT 18G: Explain your answer.

6–On a scale of one to ten, with ten being "I am confident and believe I am good at my personal development," how would you score yourself? (Circle the answer that most correctly represents how you feel about yourself).

1   2   3   4   5   6   7   8   9   10

ASSIGNMENT 18H: Explain your answer.

7–On a scale of one to ten, with ten being "I am confident and believe I am good at community service," how would you score yourself? (Circle the answer that most correctly represents how you feel about yourself).

1   2   3   4   5   6   7   8   9   10

ASSIGNMENT 18I: Explain your answer.

8–On a scale of one to ten, with ten being "I am confident and believe I am a good student (in life)," how would you score yourself? (Circle the answer that most correctly represents how you feel about yourself).

1   2   3   4   5   6   7   8   9   10

ASSIGNMENT 18J: Explain your answer.

9–On a scale of one to ten, with ten being "I am confident and believe that I am capable of having close, healthy intimate relationships," how would you score yourself? (Circle the answer that most correctly represents how you feel about yourself.)

1   2   3   4   5   6   7   8   9   10

ASSIGNMENT 18K: Explain your answer.

Through these exercises, you may be able to achieve insight into where your beliefs and struggles are and in which area your view of self-worth is strong. Very few people believe that they are all bad in every area. Through these exercises you should now have a roadmap of the areas that need focus, but don't forget to highlight the places where you're doing well. Look at them. Feel good about them. Talk about them with a supportive person. Don't let the negative things overshadow the good.

In order to find the real you, you must legitimately believe in yourself. You need to have an understanding of your own value (affirming your own self-worth). We are all of infinite worth, and it's only through life's negative experiences that we begin to question our own value. Once we reclaim

> **Once we reclaim who we are and understand our infinite worth, it is much easier to move on and form close relationship bonds.**

who we are and understand our infinite worth, it's much easier to move on and form close relationship bonds.

REFERENCES:

Gelb, M.J. *How to Think Like Leonardo daVinci*. New York: Random House, 1998.

UPROOTING STRESS

Many people going through a divorce turn to some form of behavioral crutch (e.g., physical illness, emotional outbursts, excessive use of drugs or alcohol, shopping). At the root of most misbehavior is a belief (known or unknown). If you can find the belief that leads to stress than the belief can be changed. One of the most powerful ways to deal with stress is to uproot it.

To find the person that you are meant to be, it's important to evaluate the hurtful beliefs that you have accepted as truths.

ASSIGNMENT 19: Set aside twenty minutes a day for four consecutive days. Write down how your divorce and former marriage have impacted the beliefs you have about yourself. Don't worry about punctuation or grammar, just let your mind flow without giving thought or worry to what you are writing. This process will be rewarding and surprising. By moving the pen across the paper, you are allowing your secret inner self to come bubbling out. You might encounter a lot of pain. That's okay. Keep going until the pain breaks or eases and the "aha comes. If you keep at it and reach the aha, you will have achieved a higher level of healing, freedom, and personal power.

ASSIGNMENT 20: Each day that you write about your divorce, track your emotions. You can track your emotions (e.g., sad, angry, upset, excited, happy, and worried from day to day but also from the beginning of the twenty minutes to the end.).

ASSIGNMENT 21: Which beliefs prevented you from feeling your own worth and value? Explain your answer.

ASSIGNMENT 22: Come up with a battle plan for how you won't let these beliefs prevent you from feeling your own worth and value any longer. Write the plan down here.

Uprooting Stress Process

Kenneth and Sharon Patey, founders of Growth Climate Corporation, have developed a model to help individuals under stress. Their five phases Uprooting Stress Model can be seen below.

Here is a brief description of the five phase model for Uprooting Stress.

UPROOTING STRESS MODEL

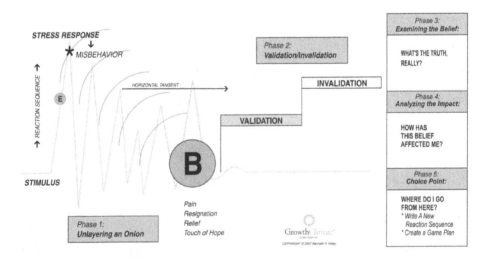

Phase 1: Unlayering the Onion

Phase one of the process understands the misbehavior (or stress response) so that you can access the belief(s) beneath your stress. As you examine your own misbehavior (it may be physical—headaches, ulcers, etc.; or emotional—depression, anxiety, etc.), you will begin to understand what triggers your physical or emotional responses. As you work through your beliefs, you will gain access to the underlying beliefs.

For example, you may become depressed every time you think about your divorce. As you begin looking at why you become depressed, you identify feelings of inadequacy. You feel like you're going to fail and that nobody will want you. As you follow this line of thinking you hit a belief—I am not worth very much and will never succeed in my relationships. While you may have never verbalized this belief out loud, it is important for you to write it down word for word. In fact, writing down all of your thoughts and feelings while unlayering your onion is a good idea. When you hit a belief, you may feel pain, resignation, relief, and possibly a touch of hope.

To give you a more concrete example of what an uprooting stress model looks like, I will share one of my own. To set the stage, at the time of this journal entry I was wrestling with whether to leave my former husband or not.

The first thing I did was to identify that I was under stress, and then I identified how it affected me. I did this by writing a conversation to myself.

May 8, 2002

I am all tied up in knots and I don't know how to let the stress out of my system.

Do what I'm taught [by Growth Climate] and become an observer, watch what is happening to me like I am merely a witness. (Now I'm going to pay attention to the physical problems I'm having.)

My stomach is twisted, my shoulders are so tight that they hunch forward. I have a nervous twitter running through my gut. My neck is weak, strained, and extremely tight. My head hurts. I'm exhausted. Don't want to do anything but sleep. I do need sleep. This current situation is overwhelming. Too much. (BELIEF)

Notice as I wrote about my physical condition, and "brain dumped" everything that was bothering me, I gradually worked myself down to a belief—"this current situation is overwhelming. Too much."

The next thing I do in this journal entry is to notice that I stated a belief and how it was affecting me.

I am telling myself it's too much and my body is reacting like it is. I am in shut down mode.

Through becoming an observer and noticing my physical conditions, I came to my belief. Instantly after hitting the belief, I am out of my focus on my physical pain and onto how that belief is affecting me.

This is a natural process. Once you learn it, you will notice that you go through it automatically in order to gain peace in your life. Once you understand the steps, you can go through them and not miss the important actions that need to be taken in order to achieve relief. After I figured out my belief and what I was doing with it, I automatically moved to the next step.

Phase 2: Validation/Invalidation

In phase two you will examine why you believe the things that you believe by making a list of reasons why your belief is true. This information is stored in the mind and filters out any other information that runs counter to the belief. That is why it's important for you to search within your heart and mind for reasons the belief isn't true.

Remember as you read my example, your reasons and validations for beliefs, and your beliefs themselves, will more than likely be very different from mine. I am putting mine in as an example to help you better see how to do it for yourself.

- I don't know what God wants from me. How am I supposed to know? How do I know what He wants will come to pass?

- I talked to a homeless person yesterday. She tried everything to protect herself, but her husband stripped it all away from her. How do I know that won't happen to me?

- How can I help her?

- What's best for me?

- Does God want me to leave my husband? So many people tell me to.

My list happened to flow this time as questions. Often it will emerge as statements. Looking at my list of questions, notice how they are an appendage to my beliefs. "This current situation is overwhelming. Too much." It's easy to see that all these doubts about what course of action I should take caused my distress.

The next step, then, is to find reasons that this belief may not be true. As this belief becomes invalidated, it is not uncommon that past experiences are finally seen as they actually occurred, without the biasing effects of filtered beliefs. In many instances, just looking for invalidation frees people from the negative beliefs they have suffered about themselves and their relationships.

The next part of my journal entry shows how I took this information and used it to recognize what I was doing and how the underlying belief caused me even more trouble. As I realized the core belief, I also started telling myself how false it was.

I keep on turning to my husband for comfort, reassurance, and peace, and what I find is more pain, hurt, and rejection. Why do I keep knocking my head against a wall? Am I playing out an old habit? Going to the abuser for nurturing. That's wrong. Sick. And yet instead of turning inward and upward I keep on doing it.

Some people feel so free after invalidating their faulty or warped beliefs that they think they're finished. Not so. Lasting change occurs when the following steps are included.

Phase #3: Examining the Beliefs

There are a number of possible outcomes when you go through phase two. One possibility is that a belief that was thought to be completely true at one time turns out to be completely false. In case where the belief turns out to be true, you will be better prepared to select an appropriate course of action. Suppose, for example, that you believed, or were beginning to believe, that a particular person was manipulative, controlling, or self-serving. If over time you found out that your fears were true, at least you could make an informed choice. Whether a belief is true or false, the greatest gift you can give yourself is to ask the question, What is the truth really? This is the most effectively done by reviewing the validation and invalidation found in phase two.

When we search for what is the truth really, we often come to our religion convictions. The answers that we receive in this search will come from that center of our being. When we pull inside ourselves to search for the truth, our consciousness, our Higher Power, our God, or whatever you want to call it, will give and offer direction.

As you read my answers to this process, recognize that they come from my beliefs and how the world works for me. Your answers will come from your frame of reference. When I write these journal entries it is as though someone else is talking to me, and I write it as such. Each person's experience will be different. The important point is that peace and healing can be achieved by tapping into our inner resources, whether that is God, in my frame of mind, or being aware of the inner self, in a different frame of mind.

In the next part of my journal I refer to myself in third person. At this point I know that my inner guidance system is taking over. Normally, when this begins to happen I enter into a space of calm, comfort, and peace.

> *Lisa, you don't trust God. Right now He has transformed into a cold, distant, uncaring, punishing person again. The walls of protection when you go into safety are up. There's no feeling, and that needs to be changed.*
>
> *(Shift in point of view after receiving the new insight.) God loves me. God will protect me as I do His will. (Shift again to answer one of my questions about the homeless girl.) Don't try to understand the paths of others. Just listen, love them, and help as you can. Trust in me (God) and I won't lead you astray. I will send people to you. Listen, learn, love, TRUST. Let go of the old lies, the hiding of your light. It's time for it to come out and shine. You are needed. God wants you to glow. Stick close to your journal. You will see the light there.*

As I examined what the truth was for me, I understood I wasn't being true to my religious convictions. My faith had lessened in having something greater than myself help me through a difficult time. This caused me to feel lost and extremely overwhelmed. I felt I had to shoulder all the responsibility myself. When I wrote this, I realized that I didn't have to worry about everything. I just had to believe that God was watching and would take care of me. This was extremely comforting for me, and once I realized I didn't have to be responsible for all things, my anxiety dissipated.

ASSIGNMENT 23: Look at the Uprooting Stress Model, then identify some of your personal stresses (physically or emotionally). Write down your thoughts and feelings that are related to the situation. Identify your beliefs and keep working to see if you can discover your core beliefs.

Phase 4: Analyzing the Impact

In phase four its time to examine how the belief that has been troubling you has affected your life. This information can be accessed by reviewing your notes from phase one. Analyze your belief by asking yourself the following questions.

ASSIGNMENT 24: Write out the answers to these questions. To get the most benefit be as thorough in your answers as possible.

How have my beliefs guided my past behaviors?

Do I need to gather more information from others to see this problem clearly?

Did I form this belief without all the information?

What have I learned by seeing my beliefs written out?

Are these beliefs connected to other beliefs I have? (e.g., not only have I felt stupid, but I also realized that I believe everyone thinks I am dumb)?

When I looked at my beliefs, I realized that I was being codependent by trying to take on everyone's problems. Of course, it was easier to worry about the homeless person than to think about my husband mistreating me and whether my marriage should end.

I also learned that I was allowing worry and stress to consume me, and I was not approaching life peacefully or with trust. For me, the answer was to let go of thinking that I needed to micro-manage everything. I needed to believe that God was in control and He would see to it that I was safe. I didn't have to obsess over details, just trust that things would be better.

I knew from this experience that I wouldn't have to suffer as many health problems or be in emotional pain if I let go of the worries and trusted that everything would be all right.

Phase 5: Choice Point

Once you have completed the first four phases, the final stage offers solutions for the future. In phase five you create a game plan, so that the next time those negative beliefs sneak into your mind you can quickly eradicate them. Your game plan should include specific things you will do the next time you have negative thoughts and feelings.

Create a protective barrier. You can place protective barriers in your environment that support your newfound efforts.

I write down positive quotes that inspire me and post them on my bathroom mirror, by my computer, on my office door, and on the refrigerator— places I will go frequently during my day. Another helpful barrier is a phrase that we teach people who come through our classes. "I don't need to go there!" Meaning, "I am not going to let this negative thought overtake my thinking." Be emotionally honest with yourself. Having already examined the belief, you know the truth. By allowing yourself to return to the same negative thoughts, you are ignoring what you have previously learned. Develop new thoughts. This way, the next time you feel negative or anxious, you have other thoughts to play in your mind. Some of the things you might consider include: memorizing something, creating as many positive thoughts

> A support system offers strength when you need it the most.

about your old belief as you can, or calling a friend so that your mind does not keep replaying the old thoughts. Include a friend in your game plan. A support system offers strength when you need it the most. Some negative beliefs are so powerful that only friends or family can give us a reality check.

Notice in the last journal entry that I ended the passage with the game plan to continue journaling, which keeps me plugged in to trust instead of worry.

When you have examined your beliefs—why you believe them and how your beliefs have impacted you—the final step of making a plan of action will help you break the negative patterns you have adopted. Uprooting stress is possible for those who are willing to go through this process.

My game plan worked well for me. I put a notebook in my purse and carried it everywhere I went. When stress or an overwhelming feeling started to take over, I would turn to my journal. My journal became my best friend. It was always available. If I could not sleep at night or woke from a nightmare, I would write until I found relief. Each time I went through the game plan process, I came up with different plans that would work to fit the situation. I was amazed how, when I turned inside and accessed this place that seemed to be beyond myself, I found peace and knowledge of what to do and how to do it. As I discovered those insights, I gained trust in the impressions that came with them. At first I doubted and wondered if I was crazy or had gone off the deep end, but as I continued to push on, I found reassuring peace.

This process became my saving grace. It helped me make my way through the confusing maze countless times. Many people told me what to do, and their suggestions ran in different directions. When the headaches came or I felt that sudden panic in the throat if I did not have my children with me, I would pull my car over to the side of the road and write for five minutes to become grounded. If I had my kids, I would see that their needs were taken care of and then disappear into the bathroom to write for a few minutes and become centered again. It was much better for all of us if that sense of peace was maintained.

Pulling in and accessing my inner compass never led me wrong. It will not lead you wrong either, if you use the steps outlined. When I fled from my husband with my six kids in

tow, I used this technique. I thought that he would kill me in a passionate rage. But that didn't happen. I wrote in my journal, received insight, and followed the inner promptings to get out. Step by step, I followed the peaceful impression. With the help of others, I got safely out.

You will be able to achieve amazing accomplishments in your own life when you tap into your internal resources. Your lesson will be different and tailored to you. It will give you the peace and answers you search for. Let's get started finding peace for you by doing these assignments:

ASSIGNMENT 25A: Validate and invalidate your experience.

List all the validations you believe are true.

1

2

3

4

5

6

7

8

9

10

Search for all the invalidations that your belief might not be true. Sometimes when you reach this point, you might immediately think, "There is nothing that proves this belief untrue. For that matter it isn't a belief, it's the truth ..." and then on and on you go about how it is the truth. Despite how right you think you are, try to come up with at least one thing that will prove your belief wrong.

1

2

3

4

HINT: Sometimes beliefs come in global language—all or nothing. "I always do stupid things." "I'll never get married again." "I always fail at relationships." If your belief is similar, it shouldn't be hard to find at least one reason that wasn't true. For example, take the belief "I'm not smart." There must have been one time in your life you got an A on a quiz, or you passed your driver's license test, or something similar that would make that belief untrue. Maybe you believe you'll never get married again. You don't know that that is the truth. You got married once, and that statistically increases your chances of marrying again. You can't prove that you won't marry again even if you say you won't. (I know what I am talking about. I got married twice after saying that I never would marry in this lifetime.) If your belief is that your relationships always fail, there might be someone you're overlooking, like a good friend or a business colleague or a client. The point is, if you look hard enough you will find something that proves your belief wrong.

ASSIGNMENT 25B: Now that you have validated and invalidated your belief, examine whether your belief is true or not. What is the truth, really? Write down your answer.

This can be the hardest and the most rewarding part of the process. To find out what the truth really is, people need to pull inside themselves and listen to their instincts instead of their heads. This can be difficult because most of us come from a culture where we live our lives with our heads and pay little attention to our instincts.

HINT: A technique that may be helpful is to take a deep breath before trying to listen. Then close your eyes, align your thoughts and feelings until you have clarity, and feel the sense of grounding and peace. Stay there and listen. Some people might have to wade through anxiety and fear, but that's okay. Be gentle, relax, and patiently wait for insights to come. When they do, they may be surprising and seem not to relate to the question or what you're searching for. That's fine. Don't worry, stay with the answer, and listen to it until it does make sense. Take the peace that comes with the answer.

ASSIGNMENT 25C: Analyze how your belief has impacted you. Make a list of how this belief has influenced your thoughts and actions. Be specific and think of all the different ways.

1

2

3

4

5 ·

6

7

8

9

10

At this point, you might be shocked at how much trouble the belief has caused you. Or you may be tempted to become depressed because you've lived this long with this troublesome belief when you didn't have to. Be gentle on yourself. Look at it this way, if you hadn't done your emotional work, you would still be afflicted with the negative belief. Now you have the chance to make changes and move forward. We cannot change the past, but we do have some control over the present and future.

ASSIGNMENT 25D: Finally, create a game plan of what you will do the next time your mind starts thinking about the negative belief. How will you stop the belief from creeping back into your life?

Do not skip this step. It is one of the most important ones. If you do not make guidelines to help keep you from reverting to the old thoughts, you will fall again.

Even if you do have a plan on how to avoid slipping, you are likely to have a mishap. But with the plan, you can climb back out faster and not stay in pain any longer than necessary. With game plans, you can build protective measures to help you realize you are slipping.

CHAPTER

7

HOW TO ACHIEVE LEGITIMATE HIGH SELF-WORTH

E
ach of us comes to a conclusion about our own worth. This is derived from our life experiences, our personalities, and our views on life. Society and our own God-given talents impact it. In Michael Gelb's book, *How to Think Like Leonardo da Vinci,* the author suggests that if we want to be successful, we should pattern our lives after successful people. It seems to be easier to implement this in our professional lives than in our close personal relationships. The reason? We are all human and make mistakes. Therefore, you may choose to pattern your life and approach to relationships after a specific someone only to find out that his or her life is falling apart. Besides that, it is hard difficult to model yourself after something as intangible as the inner personality of an individual. You cannot really see it on a consistent basis or know how the person thinks about everything, you can only know what they choose to share with you. Most successful relationships work on a deeper level, one that cannot be seen or studied by outsiders. You can copy the style and education, experience and choices of a successful businessperson. —Those are concrete and visible. Relationships, however, are invisible and delicately subtle.

93

One challenge we all face is deciding from where will we derive our sense of worth. Is it contingent upon external things, relationships, accomplishments, or something else?

The question we all must ask ourselves is, "On what do I base my sense of worth? This next assignment will help you determine the source of your self-worth.

ASSIGNMENT 26: I feel the best about myself when_____. Describe this answer in as much detail as possible. This will help you understand yourself on a much deeper level. Why do you believe this helps you feel good about yourself?

ASSIGNMENT 27: Make a list of things that you do to make you feel good about yourself. What things on this list are you currently doing? If you aren't doing any of them, it is time for you to pick one and start doing it now. You're worth it.

Common Reasons People Don't Believe In Themselves, and How You Can Avoid These Traps

Many people struggle to believe in themselves. Over the years, I have compiled a list of some of the most common reasons people think they are unworthy or think they are failures. When we have no positive feelings about our own worth, hopelessness and helplessness settle into our lives and weigh down our existence.

This reminds me of a story I heard. I was told that if you tie an elephant to a pole where it cannot travel beyond the length of the rope, and leave the elephant that way for a few months, after that time you can take the rope off and the elephant will never step outside those boundaries.

This analogy works with people, too. When we adopt beliefs about ourselves that limit our growth and potential, we have imprisoned ourselves in a small world with closed boundaries.

TEN REASONS PEOPLE DO NOT BELIEVE IN THEMSELVES

1) A lack of attachment to parental figures. People with these feelings will say something like: "My parents didn't support or encourage me. In fact, they made me feel like I wasn't good enough."

2) Bad experiences with authority figures like teachers, priests, and others. Usually the person was told, or the impression was given, that the person would not amount to much.

3) Abuse, both in childhood and/or as adults.

4) An overwhelming feeling that they are not important. Many people describe a sense of loneliness by saying that nobody cares. They often follow that statement with, "So why should I care about myself?"

5) Fear of rejection. These people made mistakes in their past and are afraid of being rejected in the present. They believe they have done so many things wrong that no one could ever possibly want to be with them.

6) A long history of attempts to achieve things that have failed for one reason or another.

7) A lack of close friends. This fosters the belief that something is wrong with them.

8) A feeling that God has rejected them.

9) A history of failed relationships.

10) A lack of ordinary social talents or visible accomplishments, such as a college degree or a high-paying job.

To help you keep in mind the **Ten Reasons People Don't Believe in Themselves** go to www.stopmarryingmistakes.com and download the **Ten Reasons People Don't Believe in Themselves Cards.**

Some of the items on the list you can't change, like being abused as a child. But you can change how you think about your history and experiences. Other items on the list include beliefs developed through hurt, loss, and rejection. Can you identify some of your personal beliefs that hinder your personal and relationship growth? It would be very helpful for you to take time to identify the reasons that you don't believe in yourself. Or even if you do believe in yourself, what can you do to strengthen your that belief?

ASSIGNMENT 28A: Write down as many things as you can think of that keep you from believing in yourself.

1

2

3

4

5

6

7

8

9

10

ASSIGNMENT 28B: What will you do to change your beliefs? Are there some things that you can-not change? If so, what can you do to stop worrying about those things that you cannot control? Be specific.

1

2

3

4

5

As you will come to see, avoiding mind traps requires that you learn how to move on with your life rather than staying anchored in the past. The longer you live in the past, the more difficult it is to move forward in your life. The things that prevent you from believing in yourself need to be resolved so that you can regain a sense of high self-worth. However, in doing this, you will need to honestly look at how you have been impacted by your past, and then create a plan to use your past to your advantage.

ASSIGNMENT 29: How can your past experiences help you in the future? Look at the list of things you wrote down from assignment 27a. How can the things that have kept you from believing in yourself help you in the future?

What You Can Do To Believe in Yourself

1. Self-worth comes from being productive. People's energy increases when they are doing positive things.

2. Self-worth increases when people help others.

3. Self-worth comes when people learn to be emotionally true and honest. They stop allowing others to hurt them. In other words, they take control of their life. It is valuing of self to not rely on others to feel valued.

4. Self-worth increases when people are in an environment that does not bring them down. No matter how good people are they need positive feedback. If they cannot find that in their current environment, they need to seek places of refuge. They need to find someone who values them and someone who they can value.

5. Self-worth comes from creating relationships and being proactive and involved with others. This increases people's ability to realize that they are of worth.

6. Self-worth comes when people are able to identify those who are healthy and those who are not.

7. Self-worth comes when people are able to detach and let go of the pain from their past. It requires them to learn more about their emotions. They learn they can heal even if the other person never says, "I'm sorry."

8. Self-worth comes from doing things people enjoy. It is necessary to fill the bucket. If a person is always giving, they will eventually get burned out. It is important to do something for the self.

9. Self-worth comes when people learn that others cannot give them their worth. They have it within themselves. As children, people learn to place value upon themselves when others (parents) give it to them. If that did not occur, they seek it from friends or others. If people do not get it there, they either give up or keep their relationships at a distance. Only when they learn that they are of worth and that others cannot give it to them do they realize that they have had the feeling of worth within themselves the whole time.

10. Self-worth increases when people get rid of their demons from the past. They can try to ignore them and hide from them but until they choose to deal with the hurts and pains of the past, they are likely to have chinks in their self-worth armor. They need to deal with and resolve the beliefs from their past.

11. Self-worth comes from realizing that one is a child of God. He loves people and He values them. They are His children. Imagine how much a parent cares for his or her children. God loves everyone much more than a person can love his or her own children. When people realize this they do not have to rely upon others for their worth.

To assist you in overcoming self-doubt, go to www.stopmarryingmistakes.com, download **What You Can Do to Believe in Yourself Handout,** and print it out to keep close as a reminder.

Through these various exercises, you learned how to pinpoint the beliefs that are hurting you, how to uproot stress to reach calm, and how to achieve legitimate high self-worth. Now that you have the foundation, you can start tackling your relationships.

CHAPTER

8

PARENTING THROUGH DIVORCE AND BEYOND

Parenting is never easy, and after divorce it seems to be especially difficult. In many cases, divorce can sever the bonds between parents and their children. Because the custodial parent finds him or herself spread thin, children often take on extra duties and responsibilities. Balancing everyday duties, parenting, and a social life seems almost impossible. On the other hand, the noncustodial parent can begin to feel like they have lost their children completely.

Divorce impacts every family member differently and has long-term consequences that cannot be ignored. Wallerstein, Lewis, and Blakeslee (2000) wrote, "Each child experiences divorce single file." Later these same authors suggest after twenty-five years of research with children of divorce that, "contrary to what we have long thought, the major impact of divorce does not occur during childhood or adolescence. Rather, it rises in adulthood as serious romantic relationships move center stage." We no longer have to question whether divorce impacts children. The evidence is clear—children of a divorce have more challenges than children whose parents stay together. Nevertheless, there are ways that parents can reduce the negative impact that divorce has on their children. That is the task of this chapter.

What to Expect from Your Child During and After Your Divorce

During a divorce many parents are unable to see the impact upon their children. In order to assist them through the divorce, it is important to help them emotionally. Remember, divorce often comes as a big surprise to them. Unlike the adults who had preparation time, even if it was just the signs of increasing distance and problems, the child is usually taken by surprise. Children will often believe they are the cause.

In order to assist your child through the divorce, it is important to help them emotionally.

Following the advice of a therapist during my divorce, I made sure that I created special times with each of my children where we could talk and listen to each other. I hired a babysitter and took each child on a walk and asked them how they were doing and what they were going through. I found that they had a hard time identifying their emotions. When I attached labels onto their feelings, "Oh, it sounds like you're very angry," I found it tremendously helpful.

I did not take their feelings personally, and I let them know that I could handle their anger toward me. It was natural. Their tension would calm. Not only did I take them on walks, with the younger children I would also hold them in my arms, look into their eyes, and tell them that I loved them and how sorry I was that they were hurting. Sometimes this method worked better when I used a dish of ice cream, which I spoon-fed them.

Since I was the one that had initiated the divorce, my children were extremely angry with me. They blamed me for upsetting their lives. There was a lot of pressure put on me to get back together with their father. I understood their anger. I told them that it was all right for them to be angry. If I were them, I'd have been angry too.

They wanted to know why I was divorcing their father. When parents confront this question, they need to be careful. Speaking badly of the other partner will only harm the children, who will more than likely still have an ongoing relationship with the other parent. We need to remember that our children are a part of the other spouse. I would tell my younger children that it was an adult thing, but I was very sad about it, and I was even angry too. I wished it could have been different for them. By normalizing their feelings I let them know that they weren't unusual for feeling anger and sadness. A few times I even let them see me cry. I needed to be careful about this because I did not want to put my emotional pain onto them, and yet I wanted to be real enough that my children knew that I was sad and angry also.

Speaking badly of the other partner will only harm the children, who will more than likely still have an ongoing relationship with their other parent.

An interesting thing that happened with my kids, and what may happen with other children of divorce, is that the children took turns acting out. As soon as one finished an ornery period, another felt free enough to go into it. It took several years before the kids stopped doing this. It was okay, though. They were going through grief. Although, I preferred for them to tell me how they felt or scream about how mad they were and how they wished I was still married to my ex-husband than to act out their frustrations later.

Another thing I did that was helpful was to encourage the kids to be physically close to me. It was hard at times because I wanted to go into my bedroom and shut out all the pressures and just cry, but they needed help. For the first six months, I drew my children closer. I opened my bedroom to them since their anxiety often manifested itself at night. At first I allowed them to sleep in bed with me, knowing that they felt anxious and scared, but after enduring a night full of bruises from all the legs and arms knocking into me, I had them sleep on the floor near the bed. This brought them comfort. Their world was falling apart, and they wanted to stay near to their mother to gain a sense of security. When their anxieties calmed, the children returned to their bedrooms on their own.

ASSIGNMENT 30: Think back to when you were getting divorced. Did you take time to be with your children and discuss their feelings safely and openly? If not, when are you going to do it? It's not too late, and it will mean a lot to the children if you take the time to see what they're going through or have gone through in the past. List when and how you plan on talking to your children.

To assist you monitoring your **Special Time Chart** go online to www. stopmarryingmistakes.com and download your **Special Time Chart**.

Common Behaviors of Children After Divorce

Some parents have a hard time understanding their strained relationship with a child even years after a divorce. It doesn't seem to make sense that their child would be mad at them for something that happened so long ago. They wonder why the child still wants them to remarry their former spouse. Why aren't they over it already? The purpose of this section is to help you identify the behaviors that you will likely see in your child as a result of your divorce. Before you continue reading, complete the following assignment.

ASSIGNMENT 31A: What specific behaviors do or did you see in your child as a direct result of your divorce?

EXAMPLE: My son closed up. He wouldn't talk with anyone about the divorce. He began hanging out with a group that I was concerned about, but I didn't know what to say because of my own issues.

ASSIGNMENT 31B: When you saw these behaviors in your child, what did you do? Did you feel like you handled the situation appropriately? What did you do that was effective and what did you do that was ineffective?

Here is a list of behaviors that you can expect from your child during and after a divorce:

Common Behavior 1: Most children want a relationship with both parents after a divorce.

In fact, researchers have found that children who maintain close and regular contact with both parents after a divorce do better academically and socially and are less likely to get involved in delinquent activity. Therefore, if you criticize your ex-spouse, you will be hurting your child. If you succeed at alienating your child from your ex-spouse, you are not helping your cause. As your children mature they will struggle in their own relationships. What have they learned—to be negative, critical, and unforgiving.

Common Behavior 2: Each child will experience the divorce in his or her unique way.

Children of the same family will often interpret the divorce and how it impacts them in completely separate ways. One reason is that each child is at a different developmental stage. A young toddler doesn't understand what a teenager does. Furthermore, toddlers, unlike teenagers, have not been exposed to all of the problems their parents have had over the years. The more stress children encounter or challenges they face during the divorce, the more difficult it will be for them to progress developmentally. For example, a teenager who is just starting to date and develop social relations may pull back from dating for fear that relationship failure is inevitable. An alternate possibility is that the teenager will turn to more delinquent behavior, such as sexual promiscuity or drugs and alcohol, to avoid the tension and frustration of their home life. In a young child, you may see regressive behavior. A child who has been potty trained may start having more accidents. A ten-year-old may act more aggressively at home or school. In many instances, although appropriate behavior has been taught, inappropriate behaviors are common to children who are experiencing stress.

My youngest was at the age to be potty trained when the divorce occurred. I held back from trying to train him, knowing he might regress. I did not think the increased pressure to learn this task would have been good for him as we were going through the transition. Even though some people think that the divorce doesn't affect the toddler, it does. Babies are sensitive to the stress that goes on around them. Often times they also have to adjust to going from one home to another. My toddler decided that he wanted to return to being a baby. That was okay. It was his way of coping.

I got out a baby cup and filled it with milk. I had him climb in my lap and I hugged him and fed him like a baby. I also put out a blanket and said, "If you're going to be a baby then you need to stay on a blanket like a baby." Every time he tried to get off the blanket I'd pick him up and put him back. "No. No. You're a baby. Babies stay on their blankets." I continued to treat him like a baby, including putting him to bed early.

To my surprise he immediately got into the role, crawling around and saying, "Mama. Mama." This lasted for two days before he decided he wanted to be a big boy again. We had no more regression after that.

From all the change that the divorce brought, he felt afraid and vulnerable and wanted to return to the time when he felt safe. Since I allowed him to do that and let him stay there as long as necessary, he eventually worked the fear out of his system and felt secure enough to encounter life again.

I believe the divorce was harder on the older children. I had many more challenges and issues to work out with them. Being an adult when my parents divorced, I know from firsthand experience that adult children can take the divorce even harder than children at younger ages.

I read research that boys are quieter than girls about their hurt. Many boys' misbehaviors surface two or three years after the divorce, leaving parents surprised and wondering what happened. It is extremely important if you have sons to get them in touch with their feelings and help them deal with this upheaval to avoid future problems.

I worked hard with my oldest son, nine at the time, who struggled silently with the divorce. He needed counseling. That was by far the best thing I ever did for our bond with each other. He was angry with me at the time of the divorce and blamed me for everything. He wouldn't even talk to me. The therapist and I worked hard with him on his feelings. Now we cherish a tender relationship. We are good friends. He thinks I'm a mind reader because I helped him identify his feelings and normalized them. When he showed signs of stress, we made a habit of meeting on the couch in my bedroom where he would curl up on my lap (he still does this even though he is bigger than me!) and talk. He resisted at first. Then his walls crumbled and he opened up. The human contact got through to him. I'm grateful I took the time to help him through those tough months. He was a quiet child, and I could easily have brushed aside his emotional needs until I was doing better myself.

One of my other children viewed me as weak since she saw her father hit me. She decided she wasn't going to be the weak one. She took the anger and power position. I figured out, that in order to be a good mom to her, I needed to let her know I was strong enough to handle whatever she tried. I could keep her safe. She tested the boundaries a lot. Once she discovered that I was not going away, and after doing some weightlifting so I was the stronger of the two of us, she settled down. I needed to be consistent, loving her and sending her value as I set the boundaries. I did not always succeed—she would be the first to tell you that. But I continued to try. We have a much more workable relationship, and she no longer thinks Mom is a pushover. We have even enjoyed some honest talks about how the divorce affected her.

I let all my children know that I'm truly sorry that they had to endure so much pain. I never wished this on them. They are strong individuals, and they can take this situation and use it to benefit their lives in the future. It is exciting to me that they are discovering how strong they are by making it through this difficult time in their lives.

Common Behavior 3: Your divorce will likely make your child skeptical of relationships.

In younger children this may not appear until late in their teenage years. However, if your divorce occurred during the teen years or early adulthood, there is a high possibility that your child may struggle with interpersonal relationships. The challenge you face will be to model a healthy relationship in subsequent relationships. One of the best ways to help children, no matter what their age, is by showing them what a positive relationship looks like. Either create one yourself, or find a loving couple that you believe to be a healthy example and arrange to have your children around them often.

I read that children do better if they have support from three different places. I decided that I would actively go out and seek this. I adopted grandparents for my children. In addition, I had the church group get involved. I also set my children up with adult teachers who taught them music, sewing, or basketball and who also taught my children that they were worthwhile individuals. I discussed with these adults my goal of creating a support system for my children and helping to show them how healthy relationships work. Many were willing to help. The additional mentoring not only blessed the lives of my children but also blessed the lives of the people who helped. We have many tender stories to attest to that. Children who get support and love from others in the community will adapt better.

Common Behavior 4: Your child may turn to others for comfort.

Often children turn to friends for support during their parents' divorce. When children do this, it can be challenging to get them to reconnect with you. It's common during the teen years to turn to friends. However, what many people ignore is the fact that most teens still desire contact with their parents, even if they don't show it.

They want to connect, but don't know how. Their emotions are raw. If you see your child turning away from you and toward others, remember that, deep inside, they still want to be close to you.

When children turn to others, it can be challenging to get them to reconnect with you.

When children turn to others, it can be challenging to get them to reconnect with you.

Common Behaviors During and After Divorce

COMMON BEHAVIOR 1:

Most children want a relationship with both parents after a divorce.

COMMON BEHAVIOR 2:

Each child will experience the divorce in his/her unique way.

COMMON BEHAVIOR 3:

Your divorce will likely make your child skeptical of relationships.

COMMON BEHAVIOR 4:

Your child may turn to others for comfort.

Go to www.stopmarryingmistakes.com to print out the **Common Behaviors of Children During Divorce Chart** to be a reminder of what to expect from your children during this time.

How to Establish and Maintain Healthy Boundaries with Your Children

Divorce often wreaks havoc on family boundaries. Children will frequently take on adult roles to help make the family function. In some instances, children will even take over the parenting role because of the devastating effects the divorce had upon the custodial parent. In such instances where healthy boundaries are lost, they are not easy to reestablish. Children who are given extra duties and responsibilities often begin to view themselves as an adult. Some grow to like that position. In most divorces, added responsibility on the children is unavoidable. Nevertheless, parents should be careful to maintain boundaries so that the child can still be a child.

Boundaries between parents and adult children are also important. Mistakenly, many people think that adult children will understand. Many children want to help their parents, but they also want a relationship with both of them. A lot of adult children are unable to take sides and may not even desire to know "the whole truth." If they are drawn into the conflict, how will they be able to support both parents without getting caught in the middle? It will be better for everyone if you keep your roles as parent and child and not smudge the boundaries.

Many ugly situations are created through divorce. One parent may try to get rid of the other parent.

When my parents divorced, I was asked to choose between them. This is not something that should ever be asked of any child. No matter the age, children feel a sense of loyalty to their parents no matter what they have done. Animosity between two parents is extremely difficult.

My ex-husband and I both communicated to our children that each one of us loved them and we were still their parents. My current husband honors the role of my ex-husband. He often tells the kids that he is not there to take the place of their dad. The children refer to him by his first name and call their father Dad. I tell the kids that they are lucky to have more people to love and who love them and take care of them. I also point out some of the pluses that kids of divorced parents have. First, they don't have to live in one house all the time, so they get a break from their father and me. This can be a bonus when they're mad at one of us. They can experience two different lifestyles, so when they grow older they have more choices to draw upon.

Establishing healthy boundaries requires that divorced parents avoid sharing too much information with their children. They don't need to know every detail of the divorce. They aren't old enough or mature enough to take in the information. Putting that heavy weight on them could rob them of their childhood. They shouldn't know about the arguments and conflicts that their parents are having. If they are exposed to it, it will cause stress and anxiety.

Maintain the rules and expectations that you had prior to the divorce. For example, if a child was expected to clean his or her room, don't give this up. During and after a divorce, children need structure more than ever.

Boundaries in Parent/Child Relationship

- Do not disclose too much information to your child.

- Avoid giving the children too much responsibility.

- Encourage your child to participate and engage in normal child play.

- Do not talk to others about your ex-spouse in front of your child.

- Maintain, as close as possible, the rules and expectations that you had prior to the divorce.

As a reminder of the boundaries a parent needs to maintain with their children while going through and healing from a divorce, go to www.stopmarrymistakes.com and go to the link for **Boundaries in Parenting**.

ASSIGNMENT 32: What are some of the things you can do to create healthy boundaries between you and your children?

1

2

3

4

5

Maintain a Close Relationship with Your Children While Your Ex-Spouse is Attacking You

For therapists, the most difficult divorces they deal with involve one or both parents attacking and putting down the ex-spouse in front of the children. Indeed, some parents are so angry and bitter that they try to turn their own children against their ex-spouse. This behavior has painful and long lasting effects on adults and children. Many people have asked their therapists, "What can I do if my ex-spouse is attacking me and turning my children against me?" While every circumstance is different, there are general elements that they can cover each time an answer is given to this question. The following section will identify ways you can maintain a close relationship (or at least *a* relationship) with your child no matter what your ex-spouse is saying about you.

Sometimes parents feel so attacked by their ex-spouse that they simply want to quit being a parent. This problem becomes more challenging when the children start reminding you of your ex. I have heard many comments that go like this: "My child is acting just like my ex and all I want to do is get away." If your child does remind you of your ex-spouse, you may want to review reaction sequences found in Chapter 2 Getting Rid of Old Baggage. When all you want to do is quit, that is the very time your child needs your love the most. The expression of love often softens the child's heart.

When all you want to do is quit, that's the very time your child needs your love the most.

ASSIGNMENT 33: What can you do to show your children that you love them? What can you do when your children display behaviors that you dislike?

Remember that if you feel like you are always defending yourself, your children are simply relaying the message that your ex wanted them to give you. Children can be easily influenced. However, they can also see the real problems even if they don't dare share their true feelings. With this in mind, consider the following suggestions on how to maintain a close relationship with your child:

5 Keys to A Close Relationship With Your Children

Key 1: Keep a Positive Attitude

Children are always trying to assign meaning to what is happening around them. If you stay positive, your child will pick up on your attitude. The alternative is to become negative and bitter. Your children won't like being around you if you're always complaining or putting down the other parent.

Key 2: Be Open and Honest with Your Child

Many people fear that they will inadvertently give their child too much information. However, if one spouse is accusing, belittling, or creating false stories, children need to know the truth. Many people become defensive when they hear things that their ex-spouse is saying about them. The defensive posture leads children and others to assume you really are guilty. Therefore, it is always a good idea to gather as much information as you can and openly admit mistakes you made. However, you should not allow misperceptions to go unchecked. This does not mean that you call your ex-spouse a liar—you simply relay the facts in a calm, non-accusatory fashion.

HINT: One technique I use, since I am not legally allowed to discuss with my children past issues concerning my ex, is to ask them questions about what they know. This helps them sort out the answers for themselves. When people come up with an answer themselves, it has a much more powerful effect.

Key 3: Take One-On-One Time with Each Child

Spend time with each of your children individually. Do this as often as you can. Do something enjoyable. Ask them about their lives and what they are doing (e.g., school, friends, work, dating, hobbies) and what they are thinking. You will want to make sure that your discussions do not always focus on tasks that need to get done or on the divorce. Maintain a positive presence in your child's life.

We call this "special time" in our house. The kids look forward to it and get creative with ideas of what to do. They love to talk when they're away from their siblings. We've gone shopping, played games, gone on walks, watched a show, gone to the video rental store together, sewed, and read.

Key 4: Show Your Children that They are Important to You

One of the biggest fears for children after a divorce is that they will be abandoned. This stems from one parent already being gone from their life, and sometimes very abruptly. As you make your child a priority they will learn to trust that you aren't going to leave. Here are examples of things that you can do to show your children that they are important to you.

A. If you say you're going to do something with them or for them, keep your promise.

B. Do nice things for your children to let them know that you are thinking about them.

C. Take time every day to hug and kiss them—even if they are teenagers. Doing this consistently lets them know that you want to connect to them. Even though they don't want to admit that they want this, it's important to them to know that parents care. They need to know on an intellectual level and also physically through appropriate touch. As you make your children a priority, they will learn to trust that you are not going to leave.

Key 5: Teach Positive Relationship Skills

One of the best things you can teach your children is positive relationship skills—forgiveness, kindness, and empathy are just a few. For example, if your children see that you have empathy for your ex-spouse, they will learn to act the same way, not only in a spousal situation but also with dates, former friends, and others. Even if you're being attacked by your ex-spouse, using statements such as, "I am sorry he/she feels that way" or "I suppose if I were in his/her shoes, I might feel that way too" or "He/she must really be hurting to say such things" can be really helpful ways to respond.

The holidays are extra hard on my ex-spouse, so we have often invited him over to our house for Thanksgiving or Christmas dinner. This helped the children to not be worried about their dad being home alone for the holidays. It also shows that we still care for each other, despite the fact that we're divorced. We act civilly and leave the past where it should be—in the past. When we're able to show compassion toward each other in awkward or hard times, it gives our children an incredible example to follow.

Show your child that you're going to parent them regardless of whether you're divorced or not.

Remember, your child's perception of the divorce will change throughout the years. Therefore, be patient and consistent. Show your child that you're going to parent them regardless of whether you're divorced or not.

5 Keys to a Close Relationship with Your Children

KEY 1: Keep a positive attitude.

KEY 2: Be open and honest with your child.

KEY 3: Take one-on-one time with each child.

KEY 4: Show your children that they're important to you.

KEY 5: Teach positive relationship skills.

To keep the **5 Keys to a Close Relationship with Your Children Chart** handy go to www.stopmarryingmistakes.com and print off the chart.

What Your Children Need Most from You During and After Your Divorce

Ironically, the thing that most children of divorce need is what has been taken from them. They need two parents.

A therapist, Dr. Kevin Skinner, shared the following with me about his experience as a child of divorced parents:

"As a child of divorce, the greatest gift that my parents gave me was that I remained a focus in their lives. My father left when I was eight-years-old. He maintained regular contact with me throughout the years. He attended my ball games as often as he could. He invited me to go on business trips with him. As I got older, he continued to be a significant part of my life by attending my activities, calling on a regular basis, and helping me financially. Even in college, my dad was a big part of my life. Although I never formally lived with my dad after the age of eight, he never stopped being my father. Last month, my father came to visit my family. As he pulled away after taking us out to dinner, I realized that I still need my dad."

This story sums up the needs of a child regardless of age. Everyone wants their parents to show love for them. I have heard men in their sixties say, "I just wish my dad could have told me that he loved me." Even if you have been through a negative experience with your ex-spouse, your children still need both of you.

I had a father who grew more distant from me as time went on because of a multitude of complex problems. Even though I am an adult, I still long for a relationship with him. I wish that he would make the effort, even now, to try to create a relationship with me. I tell many fathers that it is never too late. Children, no matter how old, cannot kill the natural desire to be loved and accepted by their parents.

Take the time to evaluate what each child needs from you. Do they require more time, more fun, more structure?

ASSIGNMENT 34: Evaluate each of your children's needs. Is there something specifically that they need from you at this point in their life? Is there something that prevents you from giving them what they require? If so, what will you do about it?

Learning how to be present and how to help your children through a divorce is not only important for them, it can also become healing for the parent. The family hurts from divorce. When the family can heal together, it can draw the fractured unit into a tighter bond than even before the divorce happened.

The Ten Commandments of Stepparenting

Commandment 1: Give the Child Personal Space

Children need to form their own identity. If you bring a child into a stepparent's home make sure your child has a place to go to be alone (personal space). If this place cannot be found in your new living arrangements then discuss this with the child.

Commandment 2: Be Yourself

The best policy is to be authentic from the beginning.

Adults need to be themselves around their new stepchildren. It is easy to get caught up in winning over their hearts. The best policy is to be authentic from the beginning. Children are good at determining who is being real with them.

Commandment 3: Set Limits and Enforce Them

It is very important for two parents to establish the family ground rules early in the new relationship. In fact, it's wise for couples to discuss these boundaries before the marriage occurs. As rules and consequences are discussed and followed, it becomes easier for parents and children to respond when something goes wrong.

Commandment 4: Allow the Children an Outlet for Feelings for the Biological Parent

Your stepchildren will always have feelings for their biological parent. To become jealous or undermine that interaction will only hurt your relationship and increase their feelings of loyalty to their natural parent.

Encourage these feelings for the biological parent. Ask your new spouse to encourage the children to have respect for you.

Commandment 5: Expect Ambivalence

Some children feel like they're betraying their biological parent if they treat a stepparent well. However, they also realize that one of their parents chose to marry you.

As a result, the child may feel torn between both parents. If you expect this to happen, it will be easier to prevent yourself from getting too defensive when your stepchild gives you the cold shoulder, doesn't respond to your advice, or criticizes you.

Commandment 6: Avoid Mealtime Misery

Common rituals can be a torment to your child. They are used to having both of their biological parents together. When a stepparent is introduced and it is mealtime, the child has a stark reminder of just how much their life has changed. The same holds true for other common rituals such as birthdays, Sunday observance, and holidays. The challenge all new families face is creating new rituals that the child can learn to enjoy. Having the child involved in new traditions can help build the bridge.

Commandment 7: Do Not Expect Instant Love

Children are slower to trust after a divorce. Most researchers suggest that a stepparent's initial role with the child should be as a friend. As trust and acceptance is gained, the role of the stepparent can change. The biological parent should handle most of the discipline.

Commandment 8: Do Not Take All the Responsibility

As the stepparent, you can easily get caught up trying to fix everything. Remember, your stepchild is still dealing with a destroyed marriage. They may not want to develop a relationship with you—at least not at the moment. Let the child do some of

> **Let the child do some of the work to maintain the relationship.**

the work to maintain the relationship. Be consistent and loving and allow the child to engage in the relationship.

Commandment 9: Be Patient

> **If you are consistent and continue to make adaptations, the children will respond favorably.**

Do not expect an instant bond. Initially, you may experience growing pains when you bring two families together. It takes time to establish boundaries, rules, and roles. Realize that there will be times when you'll be highly frustrated. In most situations, if you are consistent and continue to make adaptations, the children will respond favorably. They will realize this marriage is for real.

Commandment 10: Maintain Appropriate Marital Boundaries

> **Make sure that you maintain healthy boundaries between you, your new partner and your children.**

In every remarriage situation, it's critical that the two partners maintain their personal boundaries. As you create new interactions it's easy to fall back into old patterns. You may find yourself sharing information and frustrations with your children. They may form ideas or beliefs that can hurt your new marriage. Make sure that you maintain healthy boundaries between you, your new partner and your children.

The Ten Commandments of Step Parenting

COMMANDMENT #1: Give the Child Personal Space

COMMANDMENT #2: Be Yourself

COMMANDMENT #3: Set Limits and Enforce Them

COMMANDMENT #4: Allow the Children an Outlet for Feelings for the
Biological Parent

COMMANDMENT #5: Expect Ambivalence

COMMANDMENT #6: Avoid Mealtime Misery

COMMANDMENT #7: Do Not Expect Instant Love

COMMANDMENT #8: Do Not Take All the Responsibility

COMMANDMENT #9: Be Patient

COMMANDMENT #10: Maintain Appropriate Marital Boundaries

To keep your relationship healthy with your step-children be sure to download the **10 Commandments of Step-Parenting** at www.stopmarryingmistakes.com.

REFERENCE:

Wallerstien, J.S., and Blakeslee, S. *The Unexpected Legacy of Divorce*. New York: Hyperion, 2000.

CHAPTER 9

BREAKING THE CYCLE OF UNHEALTHY RELATIONSHIPS

I f you've been divorced, you have had at least one unhealthy relationship. Sometimes being divorced can make you feel like you've been sucked into a vortex of negativity, especially if you have been emotionally divorcing or struggling with your marriage for years. When we go through a bad divorce then find ourselves thrust back into the single world, all it takes is one or two negative experiences to leave us feeling that it's impossible to have anything but unhealthy relationships. Fortunately, there are ways you can prepare to stop the cycle before they start. In this chapter, you will learn some of the key elements that will assist you in breaking this cycle.

Red Flags

In relationships, the term red flag is used to describe a warning signal that indicates something could be really wrong. Learning to detect red flags and respond in a healthy way early in dating relationships is a valuable skill and can save both people a lot of time and heartache. This tool requires that you know what signs to look for and what they could mean to a relationship.

There are many warning signs. You probably already know that anytime someone is mistreating you or physically hurting you, it's a definite red flag. One of the best ways to know if a behavior is a problem is to trust your instincts. Below is a list of some of the most common red flags. The depth it would take to cover all warning signs is beyond the scope of this book. Keep in mind, the more a person has these poor behaviors, the more likely they are going to be abusive later on.

10 Red Flags of an Unhealthy Dating Relationship

1. BLAMING—Abusers often accept no responsibility for the problems in their lives. It is always someone else's fault. An individual who makes his or her problems out to always be someone else's fault and consistently portrays him or herself as the victim should be considered a possible source of trouble.

2. ISOLATING—A lot of abusers like to keep their victims isolated from outside influences and resources. If they keep their victims from informing anyone about their poor behavior, the victim will have a harder time escaping or being influenced by those who would try to help. Abusers have been known to hover over the victim when he or she is sitting in the doctor's office, getting a haircut, going to the mall, or even going to the grocery store.

3. GET JEALOUS—Abusers can become extremely jealous of their victims. They often accuse them of not being faithful. Some will even become upset if the victim talks to his or her friends or family too much.

4. TOOT THEIR OWN HORN—Abusers like to brag. They can go on and on about their athletic ability, academics, and good looks. These types of people look for opportunities to let their importance be known. They consider themselves one of a kind, more special, and better than others. They think they are superior to everyone else in many ways and on many different levels. If you listen carefully to their language and how they describe others it will be detectable. They also subtly put down others, including you.

5. PUT OTHERS ON THE DEFENSIVE—When an abuser feels threatened, a favorite tool of defense is a distracting or overbearing response such as becoming hypercritical, sarcastic, angry, and/or silent. An abuser is a master of twisting events and situations, manipulating a relationship, and using guilt and shame, which turns him or her into the "victim" and you into the abuser for pointing out a problem.

6. CONFUSE THEIR PARTNERS—When we deal with someone who has abusive traits, we often find ourselves feeling confused. The abuser will talk in circles purposely keeping the subject matter vague. They give us the feeling that we aren't smart enough to understand what they're saying, when in fact the abuser is not making sense and is purposely being mysterious in order to keep the listener on edge. They will say something and then later deny saying it. "You must have misunderstood," or "I was just joking."

7. AVOIDS OTHERS—Most abusers are very lonesome people. They lack the ability to emotionally connect with others. In fact, they are very good at repelling people when they get too emotionally close. Abusers don't usually have close friends.

8. TALK-IT-TO-DEATH/SILENCE—The talk-it-to-death pattern is where an abuser repeats what he or she wants you to believe so often that you end up believing that this version is what you thought all along. Alternatively, an abuser can withdraw attention, love, and approval as a form of punishment. This also gradually convinces a victim to stop standing up for him or herself out of fear the love will be withdrawn again. Remember, healthy relationships are based on truthful communication where both parties feel respected and safe enough to voice their point-of-view, be heard, and listen to each other.

Remember, healthy relationships are based on truthful communication where both parties feel respected and safe enough to voice their point-of-view, be heard, and listen to each other.

9. SETS UNREALISTIC EXPECTATIONS—Abusers set themselves up for failure in their relationships. Abusers have the expectation that others will always meet *all* their needs. When this does not happen they become upset, which normally results in abusive behaviors. Unrealistic expectations can also prevent a victim from seeing the realistic qualities in another person.

10. DR. JEKYLL AND MR. HYDE SYNDROME— In the classic Stevenson tale, Dr. Jekyll and Mr. Hyde are two names for the same person who made rapid shifts from one personality to another. The person who acts like Jekyll and Hyde changes moods quickly and there's no way to know when or how. This change can cause a lot of fear in others because they never know what they are going to get. Another form of Dr. Jekyll and Mr. Hyde is when the person acts cool, calm, and polite in public but is mean, vindictive, or violent in private.

To receive a more in depth understanding on red flags visit www.stopmarrying mistakes.com and download the e-book **Additional Red Flags Workbook.**

Evaluate your relationships for what they really are.

How can you decide if there's a problem or not? Growth Climate offers a relationship assessment tool at www.growthclimate.com to help individuals identify the red flags in their relationships. The test is an observer report of the person you're dating. It includes over 200 items identified as key issues that can lead to relationship problems. This product was developed from years of clinical experience and interviews that were conducted with divorced singles who shared their dating and marriage experiences with Growth Climate.

This test is comprehensive and covers over twenty significant relationship areas. Those who take the test receive a page report on their dating relationship. Red flags are highlighted as well as blue ribbons (meaning positive aspects of the relationship).

The questions for the test are based upon Dr. Kevin Skinner clinical experience, his research into professional literature, a review by other professionals, and a group of singles. This test has helped many of his clients, and others who have taken it, to better understand the issues that they need to work on in order to succeed.

The answers are based upon how Dr. Skinner would respond to his clients if they were to answer that way in session. For example:

QUESTION: "I have a hard time breaking up with the women I date, even if I know that the relationship isn't going anywhere."

If the answer was "always," here is the response:

When you keep a relationship going even when you know it isn't going anywhere, you are hurting yourself and the person you're dating. Unfortunately, this is common because many people would rather be in a bad relationship than in no relationship. However, many ill consequences stem from the inability to terminate a dead-end relationship. Consider the following:

1. **Time:** By keeping a relationship going that isn't going anywhere, you are wasting valuable time. This is comparable to investing in a stock that you know is going down but you are afraid to sell because of a slight hope that it might go back up. If the stock is going down and you know it, sell before you lose too much.

2. **Pain:** By keeping a relationship going, you are making yourself and your girlfriend more likely to get hurt and experience greater loss and pain. It is much easier to end a relationship early than it is to end a relationship after

many dates. In many instances, the more dates you have with a person, the more likely she is going to interpret your asking her out as a commitment.

3. The **Quicksand:** When you keep a dead-end relationship going, it can easily become quicksand. The longer you stay, the harder it is to get out. For many, it's much easier to stay than face the difficulties of breaking up. Dr. Skinner has counseled many people who have told him that they knew their relationship was not going anywhere, but because they didn't want to hurt the other person, or because they figured this was as good as they could get, they ended up marrying that person. In almost every instance, their marriage ended in divorce.

4. **Emotional dishonesty:** By staying in a relationship that isn't going anywhere you are not being honest with yourself. This type of dishonesty causes internal stress and frustration. If you choose to ignore your emotions there will come a time when you have to deal with the truth.

The best advice is to learn all you can about the person early in the dating relationship. If the people you date don't match what you need in a relationship, move on. That will keep you from wasting time. Next, you need to evaluate your feelings and emotions on a regular basis. Be honest with yourself and with the person you are dating. If you feel like you aren't ready to move forward in the relationship, don't proceed until you are. Also, take your time and really get to know the person you are dating. Far too many people run so fast that they don't take time to evaluate with whom they are running! If you get too serious too quickly, you make yourself more prone to being hurt or possibly abused.

Even if breaking up causes pain to you and the person with whom you are breaking up, it will save you much more pain down the road. This is especially true if marriage and children are involved.

If you struggle with ending relationships, you can learn to take a stand and value yourself. Many people get caught in relationships where they don't know how to say no. If this is you, the key is to commit yourself to being honest with yourself and the people you date. You can do this and still send value to the person. For example, you could end a relationship by saying, "I need to be honest and open with you about my feelings. I have been thinking a lot about our relationship and have come to the conclusion that I cannot continue it. I need you to know that I have enjoyed this relationship. You are a good person. I appreciate having had the opportunity to get to know you, but I need to stop seeing you." It is important to find something on which to compliment the person. (This should not be a problem if you chose to date them).

The best way to end a relationship is to prepare yourself before you even have the discussion. Identify your feelings and make a list of why you cannot keep the relationship going. Remember, these are your issues and you should own them. When you tell a woman that you are breaking up with her because of her behaviors, you are more prone to hurt her. If you take ownership of why you are breaking up, you will not stop the pain, but it will be easier for both of you.

In most situations, ending the relationship isn't easy. Some people will try to make you feel guilty, or they may become angry with you. If you have led them on, they deserve to have such feelings, and you should acknowledge your mistakes. Nevertheless, once you have acknowledged your mistakes, you still need to be honest. If you give in, in most instances you will regret being dishonest with yourself, and it will be harder to end the relationship the next time.

Answer to the Question:

When things go wrong in my relationships, I take all of the blame because I don't like conflict.

If the answer was "never," here is the response:

The good thing for you is that you have learned to not take the blame for things that aren't your fault. The question is: how do you respond during conflict? Do you take responsibility only for the problems you create? Do you shift the responsibility onto others? Do you act appropriately when you are in conflict?

The challenge for you won't be taking too much responsibility. It could be learning to take responsibility for the problems you create and acting appropriately during conflict.

What many people do not realize is that their response during conflict will largely determine whether their relationships will last or not. For example, if you never take responsibility for your actions, but instead accuse others, show indifference to their ideas, or become critical or demeaning, you will experience a lot of frustration in your relationships. The people you date will not be happy either.

The ideal way to deal with conflict is to take responsibility for the problems you create and allow others to take responsibility for their misconduct. For example, say you told your girlfriend that you would call her at 5:30 p.m., but you don't call her until 6:15 p.m. She yells and screams at you, telling you that you never call her when you tell her you will. Will you take responsibility? "I did call late. I'm sorry." Or will you launch into excuses or reciprocal accusations? Next, will you address her inappropriate conduct of yelling and screaming or will you ignore it? As you answer these questions, you will learn a lot about your personal approach to resolving problems.

Finally, be cautious if you find that you are dating someone who takes all of the responsibility when you are fighting, or someone who won't take any of the responsibility. Such a person doesn't know how to effectively deal with conflict. You will need to determine how to respond to people who take all or none of the responsibility during conflict. Will you let someone take all of the responsibility for the conflict even if you have contributed to the problem? Or will you let someone shift all of the conflict onto you? Your response to these questions will impact the type of people you date. For example, you may consciously choose not to date someone who doesn't take any responsibility for relationship problems, but you may be willing to date someone who takes all of the responsibility during conflicts. Or perhaps you will only date someone who will take responsibility for his or her part of the conflict. As you become more aware of how you deal with conflict and how others deal with conflict, you will realize that you are better prepared to make a decision on who to date and who not.

Many people have been glad they took the test. Some recognized potential problems and realized that their relationship didn't have much chance of succeeding. They were able to leave the relationship before investing too much time or emotional commitment. Growth Climate has received many thank you's for helping to make things clearer.

If you are thinking that you do not want to take the test because you do not want to break up, realize that the test does not necessarily lead to that. What it helps with is allowing two people to see where they are strong as a couple and where they might struggle. Two people who come from extremely different backgrounds can make a happy marriage as long as they work things out in advance and communicate openly. If two people have the same core beliefs and value systems, then it may work. If their core beliefs and value systems vary to any notable degree, the challenges will become all the more difficult.

An example of this can be found with my current husband. While we were dating and considering marriage, we reviewed the different histories of our family. We filled out our family background chart. Let's explore where there could be problems.

MY FAMILY BACKGROUND CHART

My Husband's Parents		My Parents	
Father	Mother	Father	Mother
Country of Origin			
Number of Children			
Occupation			
Years of Education			
Importance of Organized Religion			
Decision Maker			
Teaches/Disciplines			
Handles the Money			

Chart : My Family Background (pdf 147)

To fill out your own customized **Family Background Chart** go to www.stopmarryingmistakes.com and download the **Family Background Chart**.

1) Because we have dissimilar cultural backgrounds, his parents were from Canada and England and mine were from the western United States, there

was a possibility for future conflict on how we see and approach life. His parents have a different way of looking at life than mine do.

2) The number of children was not as big a difference because my current husband's mom came from a large family and was used to that culture. Doug's dad was an orphan and may have thrown an interesting twist into things.

3) Some of the biggest differences in our parents' backgrounds and how they approach life are in education and in the importance placed on religion. Think about those differences and how they may impact a marriage. Are there possible problems that could stem from the combination? What could they be?

Okay, I will give you a hint about ours. Our family cultures are vastly different. I come from a look good, standoffish culture. We were taught repeatedly to put on our halos when we were in public. We lived in a large home that was always spotless, with eight children. I mean, it was always spotless. How it remained spotless for all those years was a testimony to my mom's hard work.

My husband's roots originated in the Canadian prairies. Just in case you have not been there, let me explain what it is like—flat land that goes on forever. That is it. Farms. And a road. Total. Nothing more. My husband's roots are farmers—large families who work hard and stick together.

Now throw family reunions into the mix. Ahhhhh. My father had the attitude that they should be avoided at all costs. Relatives are a bunch of outlaws instead of in-laws. I have almost adopted that attitude. (Okay, I wish I had. The guilt gets to me.) I show up and do the two-to-three-hour-grin-on-the-face and then come up with an excuse to leave. After the duty is done I sigh appreciatively that we only do them once every three years, and not everyone comes or is invited.

My husband thinks this is horrible. His family reunions last for weeks! Can you imagine taking weeks off work to be with your family? They spend the whole time together. Unbelievable. Granted, his family is much more loving and accepting, and they want to be together. After about three hours without the computer though, I am going through withdrawal. By day two, I am looking for Prozac. Not that I don't like the people, but, for me, that is way too much time away from work.

See where a problem could develop? It's not that one of us is right and the other wrong, it's just that we come from different cultures, enjoy doing different things with our free time, and interface with our families differently.

In my family, we hardly ever stay at each other's houses because that would be an imposition. We meet for dinner at a restaurant, chat late, and call it a great visit if we're still talking to each other when it's over.

My husband's family comes to visit, stays at our home, and thinks a week is short. Yes, there are some major differences here. When my husband suggested we drive in a fifteen-passenger van for thirteen hours with six children in tow and stay with his eighty-year-old mother in her tiny house, the plan was unthinkable to me. My husband could not understand my viewpoint that such a thing would be terribly rude. He thought I was being unreasonable. Our culture and family differences led to a huge point of difference.

Because we love each other, we fought for a while. (Yes, we're normal.) Then we came up with a solution. None of us were completely happy, but we could live with it. Forget bringing the kids. I couldn't picture enduring that car ride. For me, it would have been like being trapped in a moving prison with no way out. I flew with my husband for a five-day visit—my compromise. We bought a laptop-computer for me so I could excuse myself when I couldn't take family time any longer. I'd go somewhere quiet and write for sanity.

Points of difference can reach resolutions. The more of them you have, the more energy you'll have to expend to make things work so that neither party feels stepped on. If one or the other isn't willing to put in this kind of effort, it might be a good idea to look for a partner closer to you in background and beliefs.

Ironically, many people see the red flags while dating but tend to dismiss them. They may think that the warning signs aren't really that big of a deal or will magically disappear, or that the person will change because of love. In some cases, people are so desperate to be part of a couple that they turn a blind eye to warning signs, much to their detriment. Some people don't know enough about relationships to realize that certain characteristics can hint at a much bigger problem.

I was definitely guilty of the last option during my college years. All the types of people I hadn't been exposed to before shocked me. In the midst of this new adventure a friend talked me into going to a dance. While there, I met a tall blond with whimsical curls and dark green eyes. He was funny, charming, full of energy, had an excitement for life and best of all, was an artist—a video producer. I hadn't met an artist type before and was intrigued by someone who loved to talk story as much as I did.

Flattered and interested, I continued to see him. As our time together progressed, we planned to visit his grandfather's farm. I was not feeling well and wanted to take it easy. When we arrived, he wanted me to go on a bike ride with him. When I said I really didn't feel well he grew angry and insistent. He wouldn't take no for an answer. I assumed it was because he really wanted to be with me.

As we traveled to the farm we talked about our values. He asked all the questions and I answered. He created scenarios and asked what my moral judgment was on the made-up events. I had no experience with such situations and said, "I don't know."

He grew firm and said, "I need an answer."

I shrugged. "I think that would be all right." My answer wasn't the one he wanted.

Suddenly the car veered to the right, pulling onto the shoulder. He slammed on his brakes and lurched to a stop. Before the cloud of dust could settle he screamed at me. "How could you think that? Do you really think that?" I cowed, eyes wide. He slammed his hand against the steering wheel.

My heart pounded so hard that my vision blurred. Tears trickled from my eyes as I said, "Okay, okay. You're right."

Once he was convinced that I agreed with him, he pulled the car back onto the road.

I hope this scene would create a *huge* red flag for most daters. Hopefully they would think seriously before continuing such a relationship. But it wasn't a red flag for me. In fact, I didn't think about the incident again. I excused it as a one-time slip of insanity and figured that it didn't have anything to do with what might happen in the future. Oh, how wrong I was.

Hopefully most people who are dating are more aware and pay better attention to obvious signs of trouble. Judging from the number of divorces, maybe this isn't the case. Being observant, intelligent, and honest in evaluating a relationship is important and greatly increases your chances of finding the right person.

Here is a short quiz to help you assess your knowledge of common problems in dating. Please circle the answer you feel is correct. You will find the answers at the end of this chapter.

1. Out of 100 college age students, how many report being physically abused in a dating relationship?

   a. 10

   b. 20

   c. 33

   d. 50

2. What percentage of dating abuse occurs after a couple has "fallen in love?"

   a. 40%

   b. 50%

   c. 60%

   d. 70%

   e. 80%

3. What percentage of 14–18 year old girls report being physically or sexually abused in a dating relationship?

   a. 8%

   b. 15%

   c. 20%

   d. 33%

   e. 40%

Physical and sexual abuse during a dating relationship is a major red flag of things to come. If these forms of abuse are prevalent while dating, how common are the other kinds of abuse such as emotional and verbal? How frequently do individuals use put-downs, criticism, and swearing in a dating relationship? There is no exact statistic on that, but reason would suggest it is high. Many people think that if such things happen in a dating relationship, the victim will not stay in the relationship. Sadly, all too often, the reverse is the truth. There are far too many of us who have such low self-esteem that we blame ourselves even when someone beats us. For the victim who continues to protect her abuser, extreme consequences, even death, are often the end result.

If you have been involved in an unhealthy relationship, you probably have little difficulty identifying red flags. You probably know them all, but often your common sense vanishes once you start dating someone new. It's funny how we hate being treated poorly, but we frequently gravitate to the same dangerous people over and over again.

I know a man who lives life intensely. He is passionate about everything he does. He became extremely successful in the business world. The problem came when he married an equally intense woman. The combination was explosive and led to many humdinger fights. Eventually the couple divorced. At first the man dated calm, submissive women, but he quickly grew bored until he found one more intense than his ex-wife. The couple was like a yo-yo, breaking up then making up. In the midst of one of their more disheartening breakups, the man talked to his therapist about his confusion. He made many references to how this woman seemed perfect for him, but there was just this one thing they couldn't seem to get right.

The therapist told him, "Don't you get it? You're doing the same thing again. Your instincts tell you this, but you aren't listening. A better choice would be someone with a kinder and softer personality."

"Yeah, I know but …"

He was not yet willing to see that he was addicted to unhealthy relationships. Many people who are used to unhealthy relationships find the reality of a healthy relationship—BORING. To avoid falling into the same quicksand, it's important to identify the qualities that were not working in order to put up guards.

Write down some of the red flags you honestly saw in your ex-spouse before you married. It's important to activate our reticular formation which will signal our subconscious if it appears we might be headed in the same direction. We want our subconscious and our conscious mind to warn us away from dangerous or abusive situations by admitting the red flags of our past and not denying them in our present.

Now it is your turn to start understanding the red flags that you have experienced. Take your time with these assignments. Becoming aware of these will save you lots of time in future relationships that are not healthy for you.

ASSIGNMENT 35: Identify the red flags that you saw in your ex-spouse before you were married.

1

2

3

4

5

It is surprising how many people can identify the red flags after their divorce. At this point the flags become very clear. However, many people report that they didn't see any red flags before marriage. Therefore, the following assignment is designed to get you thinking about the most common red flags that you have experienced after your divorce, or that you believe are important to watch for.

ASSIGNMENT 36A: Make a list of the most common red flags that you have experienced in your post-divorce dating, that you have experienced before your marriage, or that you have heard of others experiencing.

1

2

3

4

5

6

7

8

ASSIGNMENT 36B: Make a list of all the red flags you believe are the most critical ones to recognize.

1

2

3

4

5

6

7

8

Now that you have several lists of red flags, keep them handy to review when you're thinking about becoming serious with someone. Look to see if the person fits any of the qualities listed.

One way to break the cycle of unhealthy relationships is to learn what healthy relationships look like. The following assignment will help you determine the health of your most recent relationship by looking at the maintenance level it requires. Granted, every relationship has challenges.

ASSIGNMENT 37A: On a scale of 1 to 100, with one hundred being very challenging, how difficult was your last dating relationship? If you have not dated yet, use your former spouse as an example.

ASSIGNMENT 37B: Make a list of things to justify your answer above. Be specific!

EXAMPLE: Our relationship was a 75. Most of the time we had problems because he/she could never trust me. I was always doing or saying something wrong or like his/her ex-spouse in some way. The good times we did have were nice. They didn't last because I wasn't sure when I would do something wrong.

ASSIGNMENT 37C: What things would be happening in a relationship to justify a score below 25?

One of the most important things you can do after a divorce is to figure out what your cycle is for an unhealthy relationship. When you become aware of the red flags and how you dismiss them, you are well on your way to better relationships. Be patient with yourself. This takes time and practice.

Answers to the questions at the beginning of this chapter:

C—33% percent of college age students report physical abuse in their dating relationship.

E—80% of dating abuse occurs after the couple is "in love"

C—20% of female high school students report being physically or sexually abused between the ages of 14–18.

REFERENCES:

Fower, B. J. "The Limits of a Technical Concept of a Good Marriage: Exploring the Role of Virtue in Communication Skills." *Journal of Marital and Family Therapy*, 27, 327- 339, 2001.

Gottman, J. M. *What predicts divorce: The relationship between marital processes and marital outcomes.* Hillsdale, NJ: Lawrence Erlbaum,1994.

CHAPTER

10

MASTERING COMMUNICATION

Most therapists can count on one hand the number of couples who have come in for marital or relationship therapy who have not had a problem with communication. Almost every couple says that they have a hard time understanding each other. The standard response from them is that they do not have problems communicating. They can say exactly what they do not like and what annoys them about the other person. Getting uplifting messages across, however, seems to be much more difficult, which is understandable because it takes a lot more vulnerability and skills to do.

Verbal Communication

In order to understand communication we should evaluate the different types. Let's begin by examining our verbal messages. An important concept to understand about verbal communication is that what we say is really a very small part of our overall message. Research patterns indicate that roughly 10 percent of our communication is verbal. This leaves a whopping 90 percent as nonverbal.

ASSIGNMENT 38: Identify as many forms of nonverbal communication as you can. List both positive and negative forms of nonverbal communication.

1

2

3

4

5

6

7

8

9

10

Ironically, many of us spend a lot of time worrying about what we are going to say, though the message would be more effective if we focused on nonverbal elements such as tone of voice, physical gestures, and emotional intention.

Over the years, researchers have come to understand that nonverbal communication is directly impacted by our emotions. In fact, our emotions have a big influence on how we communicate. Let's get a better feel for this by completing the following exercise. In this assignment you will learn how your emotions come out in your nonverbal and verbal communication.

ASSIGNMENT 39: What are some of the things you do verbally and nonverbally when you are feeling the following emotions:

happiness:

sadness:

anger:

excitement:

disappointment:

Many books have been written on communication. In fact, many educational media and therapies focus on various techniques. My experience with communication has demonstrated that there are fundamental principles that make relationships succeed. Before showing you this, let's get a baseline of what you already understand.

ASSIGNMENT 40: What are the fundamental elements that make communication successful in relationships? What principles have you found that work? Why do you believe that they get a positive result when applied?

1

2

3

4

5

Using Principles in Your Communication

Growth Climate believes that two of the basic elements to effective communication are integrity and affirming worth.

Integrity

The principle of integrity applies to many circumstances. One way to break the cycle of unhealthy relationships is to include the principle of integrity in your interactions. Acting with integrity is acting with honesty and truth. Many relationships are destroyed when lies are created to cover up mistakes. When the truth is told, a deeper level of trust and intimacy is developed.

Think about it. When you come to me and tell me that you need to talk, and then from a position of honesty and regret you tell how you have messed up, there is no second-guessing. If you tell me everything you did, and I sense that you're not holding back, I don't have to speculate what is being withheld. I feel trusted, and I begin to trust you. If you come to me every time that you make a mistake and we can problem solve together, I start developing trust that you're not keeping secrets. I will know what is going on if, and when, struggles arise. It is amazing how confessing the truth *before* getting caught will enhance trust between people. Try it. Confessing the truth about something that you would instinctively hold back might not be fun at first. Ride through the storm and notice the increased trust and confidence that develops between you and the person in whom you confided. Warning: this can go extreme. Please use common sense and sensitivity in truth telling.

Being honest with yourself first, about your emotions and how you feel about a particular situation or circumstance, is important to the communication you offer in the relationship. When you are honest with yourself about how you feel, it makes it easier for you to share this openly with your significant other.

ASSIGNMENT 41: How would you describe emotional integrity?

Affirming Worth

The principle of affirming worth requires that you send value to people when you are communicating with them and not diminish them or their spirit. This is especially important to implement in relationships when you are in a disagreement or argument. Many people ask, "Is it possible to show that you value someone even if you are upset with them?" It is possible. It requires that you commit to a promise that you won't hurt the person during your conversation. If you feel yourself getting to the point where you want to say something hurtful, step back and remember your commitment. At this point you could say, "I'm getting too frustrated to discuss this issue. I do want to solve it. If I continue with this conversation I could end up hurting you. I don't want to do that." This is the type of commitment that shows that you genuinely want to value a person.

The principles of integrity and affirming worth can help in even the most difficult relationships. If you learn to apply them, you can break the cycle of unhealthy communication patterns.

ASSIGNMENT 42: What are five ways you could show someone, during an argument, that you love them? Are those ways different depending on the person?

1

2

3

4

5

While one method might work with one person, a different method might be needed for another. I have often gone to a person that is upset over something I did or did not say, and said, "I love you and I don't want to hurt our relationship. What are ways that I can show you that I still love you when we are in a disagreement?" This has worked well. After they have listed some items, I will often tell the person that I am new at showing value that way, and then I ask them to please be patient.

My current husband and I had the talk above. We know how each other gives and receives love, but that doesn't solve all the problems. I have told him about a thousand times (no exaggeration) that what I want most in the middle of a fight is for him to forget what is being said, put his arms around me, and tell me he loves me. He thinks that is a tall order. He wants to retreat. Because communicating love is important to me, he has agreed to at least try. I agreed, even though I think he should remember to gently request a hug. I tell myself he is overwhelmed and just can't keep the hug uppermost in his mind. If he weren't so overwhelmed, he would immediately want to relieve my stress. Whether that is the truth or not doesn't matter because believing it is, in itself, calming When I do request a hug it does not come out as a harsh demand or an effort to attempt to change him, it's a request that will help improve our relationship. He also makes similar requests of me. His biggest one is to resolve the agreement quickly. We each have the choice whether to honor the request or not. When we are making requests, we are informing our partner of what would be best for us in this situation and then owning the responsibility to request this behavior during the situation.

We have learned that if he hugs me and reassures me that everything will be fine then our fight ends a lot sooner than if he resists and takes a stance that he will not be controlled by me. I learned that if I state my desires clearly and give him a roadmap showing the way to solve the conflict, he is more than willing to cooperate, and I am honoring his request to get done with the disagreement. When I am successful in making my request, I put in an affirming worth statement such as "I love you so much and I need to know that we are still going to work this out. Would you please give me a hug?"

Go to www.stopmarryingmistakes.com to download your own **Affirming Worth Tracker**. This tool will aid you in developing this vital skill for healthy relationships.

Now it is time for you to apply this knowledge to your own relationship. To get started, complete the following exercise.

ASSIGNMENT 43: Talk with someone close to you with whom you are having some difficulties. Ask him or her how he or she would like to be shown love. If you are not in a close relationship, list ways in which you would like to be shown love when you are disagreeing with someone. What would help you to know that he or she cares even if you don't agree with each other?

1

2

3

4

5

Taking a Stand for Yourself in Relationships

Learning to stand up for yourself in relationships can prevent a lot of unnecessary pain. Unfortunately, many people in their attempt to be assertive end up pushing others away. The challenge is to appropriately stand up for yourself while still maintaining and developing relationship connections.

The key principle to follow is to affirm your own worth. It is easy to get caught up thinking that if you give enough, the person in question will reciprocate your love. Wrong. Wrong. Wrong. One of the most disappointing outcomes a person can ever face is when they give all they have to the relationship, and eventually the relationship still doesn't work. In learning to take a stand for yourself, start by expecting people to treat you with dignity and respect. Far too many people end up in bad relationships because they don't expect others to treat them with kindness. Learning to stand up for yourself is a critical skill that will help you break unhealthy cycles.

An excellent place that I learned this vital skill was at singles dances. I am sure that any single who has been to one of those functions knows that there are a variety of people that go. Like all first timers, I was nervous and didn't know what to expect. I walked into a dark room where lights were flashing, music blared, and I turned to talk to one of the ladies with me. Almost immediately, I felt a warm hand wrap around my wrist. The hand tugged me, and I turned around to see an older, large fellow. He smiled. "Let's dance."

I looked at my girlfriends, hoping they would save me. They just smiled and waved me on. A flood of strange feelings flowed through me. It had been years since any man other than my former husband had touched me. As I wrestled with the weird feeling that I was cheating on my ex-husband, the man asked me a question.

"Do you have children?"

I thought this would scare him away, which at the moment I desperately wanted. "Six."

He gasped. "You look so young. That's great. I love children."

The questions continued until the music stopped. I took steps to leave when he held me back. I looked down and saw that he had grabbed my arm again. He peered into my eyes and said, "Let's dance another one."

Granted, I could have said no, but I didn't. Instead I gave in, thinking, "What did I get myself into?" I was afraid that I would be stuck with this older gentleman for the rest of the night. I actually feared that because of his insistence I would end up marrying him!

Okay, fear got the best of me, but it was at that point that I realized several things: One, older men are more aggressive in going after what they want; two, if I was going to survive in this world, I would have to become better at standing up for myself. Great, I thought as I danced. I wanted to learn how to do that. After all, I didn't want to be stuck in another marriage where I continually gave into the other person in order to have peace. I could learn this. The dance would be my training ground—a cheap way to gain assertiveness training and a whole lot of real life experience.

The song ended and the hand lunged again for my wrist. This time I was prepared. "I have to visit the ladies room," I said and then rushed away. I was getting a better glimpse into how difficult it is to stand up for yourself if you are not used to doing so. It would take many more dances and many more experiences to gain the skills. I have improved, but I am still working on it, although not at singles dances anymore. This skill is not something you can grasp overnight. Never fear, experiences will be offered where you get to make the choice between standing up for yourself or continuing to do the same old thing you have always done.

There is an art in learning how to speak up for yourself without violating the other person's worth. Don't worry, life will give you many opportunities even if you do not attend singles dances. Ex-spouses and children offer many opportunities to gain experience. Even if you do not have that, there are families, work, the person at the grocery store, and the repairman who did not show up for the seventh time—you name it. This is one of those skills you either learn to grasp or you will end up suffering the consequences of not mastering it, for a long time. The sad truth is, if we allow people to take advantage of us, they will.

ASSIGNMENT 44A: As you evaluate your relationships, do you take a stand for yourself or freeze when the people you date (or marry) treat you inappropriately? Do you react and get explosive? Explain your answer.

EXAMPLE: I tend to freeze up when I feel like someone is criticizing me. Seldom am I able to think of what to say, so I just don't say anything. Then, after I've had time to think about it, I have plenty of things that I would like to say to that person. If only we all had scriptwriters!

ASSIGNMENT 44B: As you evaluate your above response, what do you do that is effective in taking a stand, or what could you do that would make you more effective?

When you take a stand for yourself appropriately there are many possible outcomes. First, as mentioned above, you can take a stand for yourself too harshly and push people away. Second, you may draw people to you because they see that you expect respect. Third, the other person may turn back on you in an attempt to out-aggression you. We must also realize that the outcome of taking a stand does not rely solely upon us. How the other person responds is also important.

Remember, the things that you can control are:

• Saying what you want to say

• Sending value to the person even as you're standing up for yourself

In the assignment below you will be asked to write at least one example of taking a stand for yourself and still sending value to the person who has offended you. Learning to do this sends a strong message to the people you date that you value yourself and that you value them. Some people will pass you by and that could be a good thing. You don't want to be stuck with people who don't value you. It's not worth the pain no matter how cute or rich they are or how lonely you are.

Once you learn to stand up for yourself, your dating life and every other relationship you are involved with will be affected. For me, when I started setting boundaries and making it clear what I was willing to put up with and what didn't work for me, I had a major reaction from my former husband, my children, family members, and even some of my friends. You see, they were used to treating me a certain way and didn't believe this new method. My former husband thought that it was just a bluff, and he set out to prove it. Come to think about it, my kids, especially the teenage ones, also considered it a bluff and so did several of my family members. If someone thinks something is a bluff, the normal reaction is to push, and keep on pushing, until the person trying to be assertive caves.

It is important to realize that once you do stand up for yourself, others may not like it. It threatens the norm and the way they are used to having things. They do not want you to be different. This is not always because they like to take advantage of you. If you change, and it is permanent, it is a guarantee that they will have to react differently. Most people hate change so they will resist it and test it.

If you are committed to having healthy relationships in the future then you must learn to appropriately stand up for yourself. You must also learn to withstand the storm of people who will attempt to force you back to your former state. If you hold strong, sooner or later the people who are resisting your changes will relent. You may lose friends, but you will gain new ones who treat you better. You are in charge of how people treat you. If you want to be treated well, now is the time to insist on it. Some people will always treat others badly. If you are stuck with someone in your life who is like that, set guidelines. You might feel as though you are not able to stop the poor treatment, although many times you actually can. You will always feel better about yourself because you took a stand. You would be amazed at how good this feels, no matter the outcome. So let's get started on having those great feelings by doing the exercises below.

ASSIGNMENT 45: Suppose that the person you're dating said something critical about you in front of his/her friends. How could you take a stand for yourself while still sending value to the person who has offended you?

Suppose someone made a critical remark about your divorce. How could you take a stand for yourself and for your former spouse?

Make a list of times this past week where you did not make a stand for yourself when you could have:

1

2

3

Make a list of times you did stand up for yourself this past week. It could be something very small. For instance, you might have stated, "I respect your opinion, but I see it differently."

1

2

3

4

5

6

NOTE: When learning how to appropriately stand up for yourself it's like any other skill. It doesn't automatically happen the first couple of times you do it. That's okay. It is a learning curve. For most people, the vital step is recognizing when they aren't standing up for themselves. For others, the important step is to recognize that they are standing up for themselves, but they are going beyond the bounds of appropriate behavior.

Don't be surprised at how many times you still swallow and don't speak up for yourself even though you're aware of the problem and are actively addressing it. You may also see yourself slam dunk anyone you think is going against you. If you're the second type of person, you'll now develop a better understanding as to why you don't have any friends. Don't get discouraged. As you learn more about yourself and how you used to respond, you'll gain the skills and courage to make different, more appropriate responses.

When you first begin standing up for yourself, if you are one of those people who never have before, your new efforts might appear rough and aggressive. On the opposite side of the coin, if you're more accustomed to being aggressive and demanding your way, you may suddenly let people walk all over you. This can be helped by training yourself to be aware of how you respond and write your responses down when you can. This will help you to gradually come to the happy medium of sending value to others while still standing up for yourself.

Give yourself a break. Like most learning skills, it takes time to find the more appropriate middle ground.

What? You mean I have to make it safe for others?

As shocking as the idea may be that you just might be the cause of some problems in your relationships, it needs to be considered. To find out how you fare, please take the following test.

Toxic Test

1. Do my dogs, cats, birds, or children run from me when they see me coming?

2. When I call people, have I ever experienced the sense that the person on the other line is not answering because they do not want to talk to me?

3. When I am in the middle of a conversation with my coworkers, do they frequently cut the conversation short, stating they need to visit the bathroom?

If you said yes to any of the questions above, this section is for you. Even if you said no to all the questions, there still might be something you could do to improve. Take no offense, please. I guarantee that there is something more you could do to make the environment around you spectacular.

Six Things You Can Do To Create a Safe Environment for Others

1. Observe your own emotional climate. Are you calm? Tense? Nervous? What message do you send out to others? It is important that you create the least stressful situation possible.

2. Look at your nonverbal communication. What are you doing physically? Are you standing too close? Too far? Are you establishing eye contact? Are you glaring? Are you threatening the other person in some way?

3. How are your questions? Are they open-ended or closed down? For example, do you ask questions that can be answered with a yes or no? Or do you ask questions that require more information and explanations in the answer?

4. Do you create an environment where the other person can process? Are you using any judgment? Do you offer solutions so the person cannot process for him or herself? If you do offer solutions, you rob people of the learning process that comes when they figure it out themselves.

5. Are you making sure the climate does not push people away? Are you being upbeat and inviting to their growth?

6. If we have betrayed their trust, have you asked them to trust again, telling them that you feel bad for the hurt that you have caused them?

I know, I know—I did not list your favorite things to establish safety in your relationships. That is okay, because for your next assignment you get to highlight them.

ASSIGNMENT 46A: Make a list of things you do to create a safe climate for others in your relationships.

1. What do you do? How does this help the relationship?

2. What do you do? How does this help the relationship?

3. What do you do? How does this help the relationship?

4. What do you do? How does this help the relationship?

5. What do you do? How does this help the relationship?

Now that you are feeling great from the good things you do to be considerate to others, it is time to look at something you do that may not be as pleasant. This is important not only for having the kinds of relationships you want but also for your own happiness.

Doing this writing exercise might be about as fun as going to the doctor, and it is definitely just as important.

ASSIGNMENT 46B: What are some of the things you do that prevent people around you from feeling safe in your company? (There may not be anything that comes to mind right away. Take some time and think about this question just to be sure. You might also want to consider asking close friends or your spouse what they experience that doesn't make them feel safe. The feedback you get from them might be extremely valuable.)

HINT: The more honest you are, the more safe people will feel around you and the better you'll feel about yourself.

1

2

3

4

5

Do you feel like the list for improvement is ever expanding? (I do!) Now that you have a few areas to focus on, let's see how well you can apply your skills to a real life scenario.

Susan and John had been dating exclusively for a few months. One day she was at a friend's house. They were surfing an online singles site looking at pictures of guys. Susan asked her friend to see if she could find John, because she knew John had previously spent time on this particular singles site. When her friend found John's picture online, she also saw that he had not deactivated his account, and in fact, he had been online in the past week.

ASSIGNMENT 47A: What would you say to John if you were Susan? What would your initial reaction be? What could you say that would be effective in taking a stand for yourself and— here is the kicker—still show John that you care about him?

How Am I Supposed to Get Along with You?

Problem-solving solutions are splattered throughout many relationship books. People often read the suggestions and agree. Then they proceed down the well-worn road of attempting to convince the person they're in conflict with to agree with them. They may say something like, "We need to problem solve, so why don't you just do it my way."

> **Not gaining adequate problem solving skills is one of the leading causes of failed relationships.**

While problem solving is often mentioned, having the actual skills to resolve conflict is rare. Not gaining adequate problem-solving skills is one of the leading causes of failed relationships.

When people who lack the right skills encounter a difficult situation, they might make a few efforts for resolution. When their efforts fail, they throw their hands in the air and quit.

Use the same scenario described above with Susan and John to work with the next assignment.

ASSIGNMENT 48: What are some things that Susan could say to both open John up and close him down?

OPEN:

CLOSE:

POSSIBLE RESPONSES:

OPEN: I saw that you're still using the online dating site. Would you like to talk about it?

CLOSE: You jerk. Why are you cheating on me and talking to other girls online? Cheater.

ASSIGNMENT 49: Think about a problem you're having in one of your relationships. It could be with a date, a family member, a child, a coworker, an employer/employee, a neighbor, someone at church or in the community. Write down the issues in a brief summary.

List ways you could address the situation with the individual that would close down that person. (Hint: this will probably be your gut response.)

1

2

3

4

5

Now list some possible ways you could address the problems and achieve an open response.

1

2

3

4

5

If you are having difficulty letting go of the closed down response, you might need to do some more work with yourself. I have found when I have a hard time sending worth to another person, a lot of times it's because I'm not sending worth to myself first. If I slow down and realize that I'm okay, and that what I want is a good thing, then I am more likely to see the other person in a kinder light. This frees me up to send worth in their direction.

Other times when I am really struggling to send worth to someone, I need to take a step back and see if I'm doing the basics. Am I sleeping? Eating right? Doing my de-stress program? Am I valuing myself? If I have the basics covered, it is much easier for me to be relaxed, mentally and physically, and then I can send worth to others.

A key element in breaking the cycle of unhealthy relationships involves problem solving. Many relationships fail because one or both people involved do not have adequate problem-solving skills. Developing the right skills in relationships is seldom taught in our society. Consequently, when people are asked how to effectively solve problems in relationships, many say I don't know. However, most individuals and couples who have been to relationship classes or marital therapy have been taught some form of communication and conflict resolution.

Here is a list of the common, and valuable, communication and conflict resolution skills taught by professionals.

1 Nondefensive listening

2 Active listening, self-restraint, and generosity

3 Self-disclosure and honesty

4 Editing and judgment

5 Techniques vs. Principles

Nondefensive Listening

Nondefensive listening helps partners focus attention on what the other person is saying in an attempt to really understand what is being communicated. This skill reduces interruptions and the desire to defend oneself while listening to the person speaking. It also prevents the listener from formulating retorts that effectively interfere with any absorption of what is being said.

One common marriage therapy technique is to teach a couple the stick rule. Whoever has the stick can talk, and the other person has to listen. The stick person has two minutes to say what's on his or her mind. When he or she gives the stick to the listener, the listener needs to restate what the first stick holder said. If he or she doesn't get it right, the first stick holder gets the stick back and rephrases what was said then passes it back to the listener to try again.

I have to admit that my husband and I have used this exercise when we were arguing and missing the point. What I was absolutely convinced of was the point of the fight that my husband had not even considered, and what the point was that he thought I had paid no attention to.

We made an agreement that whoever is the most upset gets the stick first. Instead of a stick, we used one of those triangle back pillows with a hole in the middle. We tossed the pillow back and forth. As we rotated the pillow between us, frustration grew as the other person couldn't understand the meaning behind a simple sentence. Finally, I plopped the pillow over my head and stuck out my tongue. My husband broke into laughter. After this release of tension, we were more able to let go of the anger and hear the real issues behind the words.

The interesting thing about this exercise is that we struggled, going back and forth at first. Finally, when we were getting to the nuts and bolts of the issues, we realized we were both arguing the same point but in a different language. Go figure.

Learning to communicate with each other and to decipher what the other person thinks the issue is dramatically cuts down on our disagreements.

Active Listening, Self-Restraint, and Generosity

Active listening has many different components, including the use of nonverbal communication (e.g., eye contact, nodding, adding an "uh-huh" or "um," restating what one's partner has said, and validating the partner's statements) (Gottman, 1994). One thing to clarify is that validation does not require agreement with the partner. Rather, it requires understanding another's point of view and acknowledging its legitimacy.

Self-restraint during active listening is also an important element to effective communication. The ability to encourage your partner to continue speaking requires self-discipline, especially when he or she is saying something negative or derogatory about you and/or the relationship (Fowers, 2001).

Human beings think and communicate in unique ways. I learned this the hard way. When my current husband and I were first married, it took us forever to figure out why we continued to have conversation interruption violations. As we worked through it, we came to a realization—women and men talk at different speeds. Whenever I thought my husband was finished talking, I would start. He would be offended because he did not get to finish what he had planned to say. I realized that when he pauses that does not mean he is done, that just means that he is accessing more data. I have learned that when things are tense between us then I should first count to fifteen, and if he has not said anything then I should ask if he is done or if it is my turn since I am not clear about when it is.

On the flip side, he has learned that I grow impatient and irritable if I think he is launching into a long lecture. I have asked permission to tell him when I'm getting lost. I will plead, "Stop. I can't keep track of all that. I'm confused. Pick one thing."

Sometimes it takes so long for us to understand each other that we just give up, confirm that we love each other, and go watch Family Feud instead of wasting any more time fighting. We have learned to let some things go.

The trick is to come up with a way that works for you. Pay attention where problems arise in your dialogue. We've found that my husband likes to ask questions. When I hear him ask a question, I'm prepared to answer. He wants to keep on talking. I become frustrated because I want to answer him, and he becomes frustrated when I jump in to answer because he didn't mean for me to answer. He was using a rhetorical question to frame his argument. We have yet to come up with a solution. Any input is welcome.

Another good problem solving skill to use is generosity, or the act of using active listening to encourage your partner to speak. By doing this, you give a gift of attention and interest. When people feel they will be listened to, they are much more likely to open up and share their thoughts and feelings.

Self-disclosure and Honesty

Self-disclosure can be risky during a conversation or argument. Those who have been hurt when they tell their partner what they feel will seldom try a second time. However, if no important information is ever shared about self, a relationship will not grow and most of the time it deteriorates.

All good relationships require honesty. When trust is part of the relationship it's easier to disclose personal thoughts and feelings. Without honesty in the communication process little can be accomplished to solve problems, primarily because the foundation for discussion is then built upon faulty assumptions.

A therapist told me the following story: The husband of one of my clients sat her down one day and told her that he was addicted to pornography. After overcoming the shock of this disclosure, she arrived at some realizations. First, her husband had confessed this behavior and, second, he did so early in its manifestation. Although she did not like what he was involved with, she at least felt certain she could trust him to tell her the truth. After that, the couple sat down together and engineered a game plan that would support her husband and help him resist temptation in the future. Because her husband had told her early and she was willing to work with him, the couple grew closer.

Just imagine if shame prevented the husband from making a confession to his wife. What would have happened to the relationship? If the wife found out on her own then trust would be eroded. Even if the wife didn't discover what was going on, there would be a sense of distance that would drive an invisible wedge between them. All areas of intimacy would be affected.

Editing and Judgment

The concept of editing refers to how an individual decides what to say and what not to say. This requires that an individual know how to resist saying things that could harm the relationship. It also requires a level of self-awareness to edit what one says when conflict or tension is high.

Judgment, or practical wisdom, is a key element of effective communication. Knowing when to say something and when to keep quiet is challenging. Knowing what to say or when to say it is a judgment issue. Unfortunately, this judgment is often disregarded in the heat of the moment. Continual day-to-day experience helps us base that judgment on our familiarity and knowledge of our partner.

I have a friend whose husband stays away from her when he's stressed. The first time she experienced this was when they were dating, and he received some particularly bad news. Wanting to be the comforter, she rushed to his side to hug him. He separated from her saying, "Don't touch me."

She responded to his troubles in the way she would want to be treated. When she receives bad news, she wants her partner to take her in his arms and tell her things will be all right. His natural response when she is under stress is to leave her alone. At the beginning of their marriage she was offended. "He runs away when I need him the most. Typical."

After working it out, they decided the best way to show their love was to figure out how the other person understands love and give that kind to them. The lady in the above story thought hugging was the answer, but she learned to give her husband space when he was stressed. The husband thought he should leave his wife alone when she was upset, but he learned to hold her and reassure her. Using your instincts and being open to new ideas and methods is important.

Techniques vs. Principles

The list above includes many techniques about how to solve problems. Indeed, researchers have found that these basic skills can help couples break unhealthy communication patterns. However, real lasting change requires more: you must understand that techniques alone do not create change. Principle creates change. The techniques above will only work if the people using them also apply principles to the skill set.

Principles are fundamental laws. For example, honesty as described above is not a technique. It is a principle which should lead to a healthy relationship. Relationships without principles have a hard time surviving.

Even if one person uses principles, it doesn't guarantee that the relationship will last. Suppose you told your boy/girlfriend that you had a sexual relationship with someone after your divorce, and from that point on your new partner used that information against you. Does this mean that you did the wrong thing in disclosing your information? No. Many people would say yes, but I disagree. If your new love interest punishes you for this type of honesty, he or she will probably find other things about you that they don't like. It isn't your honesty that created the problem, it was an inability to forgive and a lack of relationship skills. Either a relationship is going to be based on truth or it isn't. If people cannot recognize the integrity and humility in the act of confession and honesty but instead use it as a weapon, this indicates a problem with character. A good relationship cannot be built on such a foundation.

Some people will leave out part of the truth in confession or exaggerate their action or behavior to make themselves look good. In the process, the truth is lost. Such couples not only have to worry about the original issue, they also must deal with the manipulations and false techniques their partner is using to mask the truth.

When principles are used in communication, problem solving becomes much easier. If both partners are committed to honesty, and they know from proven experience that their partner will tell them the truth no matter how difficult it is, then there is much less tension and stress in resolving the conflict.

ASSIGNMENT 50: What are some of the principles that make communication effective?

1

2

3

4

5

ASSIGNMENT 51: List the areas where you use principles in your relationships. Which principles? How does that work for you?

1

2

3

4

5

List areas where you could improve the application of principles in your relationships.

1

2

3

4

5

How do you plan to go about changing it?

List action steps that you are going to take in the next week.

1

2

3

4

5

Imagine what your life would be like if you used the above mentioned principles. Describe in as much detail as possible what that would look, feel, and be like.

Trusting Others

Unfortunately, a bad marriage and divorce can warp our perception of people and relationships. Generally speaking, those of us who have been through a difficult marriage and/or divorce tend to be less trusting and have an increased fear that we will be hurt in relationships. Instead of being able to trust others, skepticism settles in because of the

Unless we learn to trust others, at least those who are safe, we will miss out on an important part of the healing process.

pain we experienced. This is completely understandable and is a normal reaction to pain. However, avoidance does have its downside. Unless we learn to trust others, at least those who are safe, we will be missing out on an important part of the healing process.

The final assignments in this section will help you to start trusting others and also aid you in identifying outside resources that can help.

ASSIGNMENT 52: List at least five people who support and care about you. Identify how they have aided you. Then find a way to express your thanks to them for their assistance.

1)

2)

3)

4)

5)

NOTE: If you cannot think of five people, include individuals that you would like to get to know better who you think could support you if they knew your circumstances.

Trusting Again

When you have endured a divorce, one of the most challenging things you will experience is learning to trust. One client who came to see me after her divorce grew intensely uncomfortable when someone showed interest in dating her. She would escape the situation as fast as she could. Then she would flop on her bed, pull out her journal, and list everything she could think of to prove how this man was similar to her ex-husband.

She thought this technique kept her safe from making the same mistakes, and no doubt it did. The problem with looking at all men as a potential *big mistake* or *pain causer* is the We end up distancing ourselves from everyone—even those who could bring happiness into our lives. When my client retreated into her shell, she also isolated herself and increased her pain, her loneliness, and her feelings of being misunderstood. This actually made it more difficult for others to support her, even those sympathetic to her plight. In a climate like this, it doesn't take long for deep depression to gain a foothold. Self-imposed isolation can create a toxic environment. When people aren't interacting with others, they sometimes become stuck and stifled in their own beliefs and miss out on the opportunity and growth potential of being challenged by others. Efforts at balance are important.

> **The only way out of this dilemma— and the only way to avoid it in the first place—is to learn how to create new relationships and trust again.**

The only way out of this dilemma—and the only way to avoid it in the first place—is to learn how to create new relationships and how to trust again. This may take time. You don't have to engage in new relationships overnight; however, it should become a goal.

For those of you who are struggling in this area, maybe my experience will help. At one time in my life I was so shut down and afraid of people that the thought of talking to new people terrified me. I remember being challenged to talk to someone the next time I stood in line at the grocery store. I thought, "No way, I'm not going to do that. What would I say? What if they follow me out of the store and attack me?" My worries soared.

Now, you may be identifying with my fear, or you may be thinking that I was messed up and you're laughing at me for having a hard time believing that something as simple as talking to a stranger would cause such a reaction. In either case, I'm okay if you think this is strange behavior, because the point is that I did have a horrible time extending myself to others. I saw it as being stupid and asking for more hurt. Like most people I don't like pain, so I avoided what I thought would cause pain—other people.

It took me a long time before I could talk to strangers. I started out easy by sitting next to someone who looked like they would have difficulty killing a fly. I would say hi, and, to my surprise, a conversation would sprout.

As I continued to do this it became easier. I still remember the day I realized I had talked to the cashier for five minutes and was smiling because of something she said. What a surprise—I was the one who opened my mouth first.

Establishing relationships and reaching out to others can be done. It is not as difficult as it seems. Nowadays, I give speeches, I talk on the radio and TV, and I meet a lot of different people at events. If I can laugh on the radio and converse easily in front of many people even though I was once terrified to say hi to someone in line at a grocery store, you can connect with others also. Take it one step at a time. Here is your chance to explore what environments will work best for you to open up and meet some new people.

ASSIGNMENT 53: Make a list of places where you can meet new people. This list doesn't have to have anything to do with romance. It could be a possible new friend, colleague, or peer. It could also be someone who is interested in a similar hobby as you.

1

2

3

4

5

6

7

8

9

10

Although divorce is not a fun thing to go through, it is not a death sentence. Anyone can pick up the pieces and put their life back together. It will be different than the life you lived before, and it can be rewarding and enriching. Be gentle and patient. This is a process, not a destination, and there is much to learn from the journey.

Although divorce is not a fun thing to go through, it is not a death sentence.

Taking Off the Blinders

Many people admit that they put blinders on during the weeks/months they're dating. One way to take the blinders off is to step back, and objectively evaluate what is happening in relationships. Remember that every individual and every relationship has a climate. As you observe each of your relationships, you will feel the climate. If you cannot assess what the climate is, you need to gather more data. Here are some examples of climates in relationships.

- I feel like I'm walking on eggshells each time I tell him/her how I feel.

- I enjoy every moment we are together.

- I feel overwhelmed and exhausted.

- I feel comfortable.

- I am uneasy with this person.

- I feel safe.

- I do not feel comfortable with him/her meeting my family or friends.

As you hone your skills at observation, you will soon see that every relationship really does have a palpable climate. There are many reasons why some people would disregard or ignore the information they receive. For example, some people have such a strong desire to be in a relationship that they ignore the instinct telling them that something could be wrong. Other people struggle to recognize the factors that could lead to relationship problems because of their background. In other words, they grew up in an environment that was just like their dating relationship. This brings up the point that some upbringings are extremely dysfunctional. It is harder for these people to recognize warning signs. There are also people who get into unhealthy relationships and ignore the problems they're having because they don't believe they deserve better.

> **If we want to break the cycle of unhealthy relationships, then we need to evaluate our associations for what they really are by honestly assessing the climate.**

Though there are many reasons why we sometimes don't pay attention to the climate around us, if we want to break the cycle of unhealthy relationships, then we need to evaluate our associations for what they really are by honestly assessing the climate.

ASSIGNMENT 54: If you're dating, identify some of the climates that you have felt in your relationship. Take some time to evaluate at least one relationship (not necessarily a dating relationship) you have been a part of during the past few months.

Another great way to get a handle on the relationship's climate is to ask your friends, family, neighbors, and children what they feel when you and the person you're dating are together? Do they want to be around this person? What do they think of the other person? What do they sense the general feeling is when they're around you two as a couple? Friends can have great insight, but sometimes they can be biased. Some have their own issues or motives—like not wanting you to get caught up with someone because then you will not be available for them as much, or wanting you to get into a relationship because you're bugging them. Either way, the results of the talk can be biased. That is why it's a good idea to ask a lot of people so you can get a general overall feeling and weed out these biased opinions.

NOTE: Children can be a great indicator of the type of climate that exists. They have a natural ability to sense the undertones that adults cannot. Here again is a word of caution: some children will not like anyone because they represent the end of your relationship with their biological parent. Other children will accept anyone, just as long as you hurry up and marry them.

Although it might feel like nothing will ever be normal again after a divorce, it can happen. To accelerate your healing, make sure not to isolate yourself. Put yourself in healing environments, and watch how you frame your divorce to yourself and others. Gluing your life back together is possible and can have many enriching rewards.

REFERENCES:

Gottman, J. M. *What predicts divorce: The relationship between marital processes and marital outcomes.* Hillsdale, NJ: Lawrence Erlbaum, 1994.

Fower, B.J. "The limits of a technical concept of a good marriage: Exploring the role of virtue in communication skills." *Journal of Marital and Family Therapy,* 27, 327–339, 2001.

CHAPTER

11

DATING AFTER DIVORCE

R eentering the dating game after divorce is seldom easy. Many of us feel awkward. Our identity as a married person is abruptly gone, and we are starting the arduous process of redefining ourselves, not only to the world but, most importantly, to ourselves. We question whether anyone will want to be with us, especially if we feel like damaged goods. Add children to this picture and many of us resign ourselves to the idea of being alone for the rest of our lives.

We wonder if we're prepared to date or whether we even want to date. We get anxious about how we'll meet new people. We wonder if it's a good idea to let someone else into our lives again. Some of us swear off the opposite sex completely. We become adamant in our assertions that the risks aren't worth it, and we'll be perfectly content living alone. We embrace our independence. A large percentage of us fear that we'll hurt our children if we date, and we even fear that we're being selfish for considering the possibility. Haven't our children been through enough pain from the divorce? We certainly don't want to expose them to any more pain. Then there are those of us who fear that if we don't get remarried and provide a mother/father figure for our children then their lives will be irrevocably damaged. Needless to say, dating after divorce is challenging.

177

Ironically, these fears fade away for most people as they find their way into new relationships. Remarriage is so popular that about seventy-five percent of younger divorced individuals do remarry (Olsen & DeFrain, 1994).

Phases of Dating After Divorce

Just like most experiences in life, dating after divorce has different phases. Each individual has his or her own unique dating experiences. Some of us can hardly wait to start meeting new people and forming a new relationship. Others are much more reserved and question whether they want a new relationship. Here is an outline of some of the phases that people can experience when dating after divorce.

Phase I: Do I Have To Do This Again? Or ... Let's Get The Show On The Road!

In many cases, the initial phase of dating after divorce is intimidating. A lot of people try to put thoughts of dating out of their mind. But after time passes, nagging friends, family, neighbors, church members, or loneliness set in and thoughts turn to the possibility of venturing into the unknown journey called dating.

A common roadblock for many people happens when considering a relationship with anyone other than the person they were married to. Although they know that it isn't, it feels like cheating. Another facet of this particular hang-up is that some people just aren't ready to let go of their now defunct relationship. They continue to indulge in the hope, belief, and faith that if they remain faithful, the relationship will somehow work itself out.

I have seen people in this type of thinking go to extremes, performing makeovers on their personality, flaws, and habits. People caught up in the desire to recapture what once was will often call their former spouse and get an actual list of things to do which, they hope, will get them back together. Such people probably don't have the desire to explore new relationships. I've seen this type of dedication and determination work, and the couple remarried. Some are still claiming that their marriage is now happy, and the changes they made were all that was needed to fix things. More often, it is a hopeless exercise in futility. Generally, when a divorce is final it's best to let go and move on.

After enough time, most people grow tried of pining after their former mate, and they begin to look around and wonder what it would be like to go on a date with someone else.

There are others who just don't want to deal with the hassle of relationships again. "The first one was bad enough," is their attitude. They aren't looking, and they don't want to look.

These people can have happy lives and enjoy the way things are. They don't want to be bothered with that relationship mess. Others have become bitter and refuse to date because they believe that no one is good enough. Eventually, a good portion of these people, no matter where their attitudes have been, start wondering if they can find a person who will accept them, adore them, love them. Could they be happier with someone other than their ex-mate? Should they give it a try? If they do give it a try, how will they go about it? How do you meet someone? It's not like single people stand around the mall carrying a poster unequivocally stating, "Single and your next spouse. You will find eternal bliss with me—guaranteed." (Although, I have to admit that would be nice, and it would take the frustration out of dating.)

Some of us think, "Do I have to do this again?" This feeling comes from not knowing what lies ahead. Our mind likes to know the outcome, or expected outcome, of a journey. Entering the dating game after an extended leave of absence is a universe of unknown outcomes. Many divorced people can't help remembering all the negativity they experienced with their ex-spouse. They've internalized the negative experiences from their marriage and now fear that the people they date will treat them in a similar way.

Eventually, however, as they experiment with new relationships and find that others can treat them with kindness and respect, they begin to have renewed hope. At this point, the initial state of fear and concern dissipates, and dating becomes more comfortable.

Let's get the show on the road!

There's another group of people, and they simply cannot wait for their marriage to be over. They've been emotionally divorced for months or years. Some of them are out searching for a new partner before the judge has time to sign the final papers. Being alone and single just isn't an option. I have heard stories about people who engage in four or five dates a week—all with different people. Those who fit in this category are seldom single for very long. These are men and women who want to jump back into dating.

I admit that, between the two groups, I was in the "Let's get the show on the road!" group. I had mourned the conditions of my marriage for years. I had cried thousands of tears. By the time the judge finally signed the papers I was ready to celebrate—my mourning period was over. To anyone shocked by that statement, anyone who thinks that perhaps I didn't value my marriage, remember that I was in an abusive situation, and by the time I got out I felt like I had escaped from a concentration camp. Things were so bad for me that getting out was like being given a whole new life to live over. I know many others in similar circumstances who feel the same way.

Things were so bad for me that getting out was like being given a whole new life to live over.

Of course, I didn't do the four to five dates a week. I had children and responsibilities. I did, however, go to dances and surf the Internet. This brings me to a warning for those who have children and do like the thrill and adventure of dating. Family comes first. If you leave your children constantly, you are neglecting them and failing in your parental responsibilities. Don't go there. I have friends whose children grew angry and rebellious over being left alone so much while their parent gallivanted off on dates. It isn't worth it. A helpful guideline I used before accepting any date was to determine if the person asking me out was worth leaving my children for the evening. Often the answer was no. When the answer was, "I would really like to explore the possibility of this

> **Determine whether the person who asked you out is worth the price of leaving your children for the evening.**

relationship," I scheduled the date for after the children were in bed, paid my oldest child well for babysitting, and kept my cell phone with me. I also asked neighbors who were friends to keep an eye on the house. If the fellow had a problem with this, I had my answer on how things were going to work out, and I moved on.

Determine whether the person who asked you out is worth the price of leaving your children for the evening.

Now, back to why someone would leap quickly from a bad marriage into the dating world. Well, for me, it's because I am a hopeless romantic. I have always harbored this dream of being married to a Romeo who loves me. Not only would he love me desperately, but also adore me and understand who I really am and treasure that. This dream of Romeo protected me through the abusive episodes in my early childhood. I knew that sooner or later Romeo would find me. He would be angry about the terrible treatment I had received, and he would magically make it all better.

Okay, stop laughing. I know it sounds silly, but that little girl fantasy stayed with me through all those years. It became clearer in details and it rematerialized, whispering its old promise in my ear, once the divorce was complete and I had a second to catch my breath. Maybe I didn't find Romeo the first time, but there was a chance of getting it right the second go around— actually, more than a chance, because I had been through enough. God would send me Romeo now because I had definitely earned my stripes.

At first, when I thought about dating it was a hesitant idea. I thought I would try out the Internet to see what it was like because I had heard of so many success stories there. Maybe I'd go to a dance and get a taste, but *wow*, once I was there I was hooked. Major adrenaline rush!

Dances and the Internet allowed me an escape from my mounting problems. Having men compliment me, pay attention to me, and wanting to hear what I had to say provided quite the rush, especially to a person who had been a stay-at-home mom and pregnant for the past ten years.

I was a romantic, and I knew Romeo was just around the corner. If I stayed home night after night, I was living in fear and not making myself available for what I knew would make my life and my children's lives perfect.

Okay, I am being dramatic, I admit, but I hope that I'm getting my point across. Dr. Skinner would say that I used the idea of romance as a cover-up for the fact that I didn't feel comfortable with myself. Discomfort was driving me back into a relationship because I believed that if I didn't have a spouse then I wasn't okay, or that something was wrong with me. I would say to him, "You're right."

The reason I know he was right is that I recognized something about my personality: When I am alone for extended periods of time, I get anxious. I feel like something is wrong. I look to others to validate me and tell me that I am all right. I tried to give up my dating and Internet dating cold turkey. Now I know what cold sweats and withdrawal feel like. Not conversing with men and not playing the single dating game felt like something was wrong, missing. I needed it to feel good. I would try to refrain all day, but by the end of Sunday I would think, just five minutes on the Internet to see if I got any flirts. The next thing I knew I was talking on a phone and then going to a seminar for singles. These, of course, are all classic signs of people who rush into marriage.

After arguing the value of romance and Romeo and all that, I must admit that the problem with this approach is that if we don't give ourselves time to get established and get on our own feet as a single person, we'll never know that we can make it in this world on our own. We'll struggle with our identity endlessly because we haven't taken enough time to figure out who we really are.

After realizing that I was guilty of this, after much soul-searching and study, I came up with a policy that might be helpful for others. I was not going to remarry until I was okay not getting married. When I came to the point where I could focus on other things and be okay with just having friends, then I knew that remarriage, with the right person when the right situation came along, would be a good thing. Amazingly, by the time the right man finally came along I valued the merits of being single so much that I wasn't sure I wanted to get remarried at all. Go figure.

Phase II: I Guess This Isn't So Bad. Or ... Back In The Saddle Again!

Once the initial fear of dating finally subsides, many of us find that we are actually enjoying ourselves. It's nice to spend time with someone without conflict. It can also be refreshing to spend time with those who are in similar situations. Being with other individuals who understand the pressures, the custody problems, and the adjustment struggles can act like a balm to the hurting soul. During this phase, our minds often shift from constantly thinking about our past marriage to thinking about new prospects, new problems, and new possibilities. There may still be days where the past can occupy the mind, but they are fewer in number.

For some, this phase is helpful in that it allows them to slowly make new friends. These people are not in a hurry. They meet others on their own or with the help of friends, family, and coworkers.

It's unfortunate that some of us get so caught up in finding someone that we impulsively jump into another marriage without giving it proper thought and

○∽○

Being with other divorced people who understand the pressures, the custody problems, and the adjustment struggles can act like a balm to the hurting soul.

consideration. Sometimes this is called rebound marriage. Seldom do quick remarriages work. Unresolved issues from the past often get in the way of developing and forging healthy relationship patterns with the new spouse. There must be grieving, anger, and healing time between marriages in order for us to avoid taking the issues from one relationship and projecting them directly onto the new one.

Phase III: Getting More Serious? Or ... I'm Tired of Trying

Before phase three starts, some people are already remarried. This is especially true of men. After a divorce, men tend to remarry sooner than women. A high percentage of divorced people (men and women) are remarried within five years of their divorce. ("For Richer or Poorer", Illustration By Sarah Wilkins, in January/February 2005 issue of Mother Jones. Quoted in a posting from Smart Marriages Listserv on Jan. 4, 2005.) The formation of new relationships for both men and women happens very quickly, although not all of these relationships end in marriage. It's not uncommon for divorced singles to develop many close relationships before they settle down with one person. The challenge isn't in getting serious, it's working out all the details (children, finances, unresolved issues, unexpected emotional triggers, how to deal with a former spouse, etc.). Eventually, divorcees find someone with whom they can solve these dilemmas.

There is another group. These people stay single for extended periods of time. Initially, the pain and hurt cause them to be non-trusting. When they do try dating and get hurt again, they pull the quick trigger (meaning put an end) to the newly forming relationship. The fear of being wounded is so real that they often quit dating altogether. This group may choose to never remarry, or they try dating halfheartedly, but their worries prevent them from giving dating a fair chance. A lot of these people won't admit that the reason they're not dating is due to fear. Most of them fool even themselves. They will say things such as, "There's no good man/woman left." Or "I will get married when the right person comes along." When they say this, they fully expect it will never happen. Some say that they're happy being single. Why would they want to put themselves through all that misery again?

> **The fear of being wounded is so real that they often quit dating altogether.**

Some of these people are truly fine being single and on their own. They are independent and would value a relationship if all the right factors fell into place. Many others who make these claims are not happy. They live like frightened hermits, hoping nothing will find and hurt them.

Phases of Dating After Divorce

PHASE I: Do I Have To Do This Again? Or … Let's Get The Show On The Road!

PHASE II: I Guess This Isn't So Bad. Or … Back In The Saddle Again!

PHASE III: Getting More Serious? Or … I'm Tired of Trying.

ASSIGNMENT 55: Review the phases. Do you see yourself in one of them? If so, which phase are you in? Describe what it is like.

ASSIGNMENT 56: Do you know others who have had the direct opposite response to dating than you? Write what it must be like to have their mindset.

Did you learn anything about yourself or the other person with the different mindset by looking from varying perspectives at situations that are similar? How can this knowledge help you to socialize with other singles as you date?

Evaluating Your Strengths and Weaknesses

If you had to assess your own strengths and weaknesses in relationships, could you do it? What are your strengths? What are your good qualities? What are the areas that need improvement? In this section, you will be asked to complete a self-evaluation. An honest evaluation can be humbling. Dr. Skinner says that when people do this emotional work, his experience has shown that they succeed more often because of the time and effort they put into evaluating themselves.

Those who seek new knowledge and learn how to implement that knowledge often succeed in relationships.

ASSIGNMENT 57A: List at least five of the best qualities that you bring to a relationship.

1

2

3

4

5

ASSIGNMENT 57B: Give examples of how you have used those qualities to strengthen your relationships.

1

2

3

ASSIGNMENT 58A: List at least five things that you would identify as your weaknesses in relationships.

1

2

3

4

5

ASSIGNMENT 58B: Evaluate each of the weaknesses listed above. What do you think you can you do to eliminate each of these issues? Take your time and be specific. Make sure you include exact steps for how you are going to accomplish it.

EXAMPLE: I am too negative and critical. I need to be more positive. I am going to try and communicate positive things rather than complaining or being negative. I will do this by keeping track in a notebook of every time I am negative. I will continue to mark until I can go a whole twenty-four hours with people around and not criticize one thing.

How do you connect?

When children are born they have a general temperament. Their temperament is altered by their environment. Children who adjust and feel safe are likely to develop healthy relationships. Researchers have found that children who grow up in secure family relationships are more likely to develop secure attachments during their adulthood. The reality is that not everyone grows up in a safe environment where they can securely attach to an adult. Such individuals can still learn, but they need to know how to implement the characteristics of those who are secure in relationships.

There are common styles that are more conducive to successful relationships. How we attach or don't attach can have a huge impact on the outcome of our interactions. So how do you relate? Let's find out. There are three types. No one fits neatly in one category, but a person does lean toward one area more than the other.

Attachment Style Type 1: Secure

The first type of attachment style is secure. The secure adult can be characterized as embodying trust, friendship, and positive emotions. Secure adults also believe in enduring love, generally trust in others, and are confident in the self and its likability. These individuals are also more likely to succeed in their relationships, and they believe in the general goodness of relationships. Their key qualities include:

1. Developing trusting relationships and friendships.

2. Having genuine self-confidence.

3. Believing in enduring love.

4. Being a positive person.

5. Creating a positive environment in relationships.

Those who have these qualities find relationships relatively easy. They are comfortable getting close to others. They feel comfortable depending on people and having people do the same for them. They don't often worry about being abandoned or someone getting too close to them.

Attachment Style 2: Avoidant

The next relationship style is avoidant. These individuals almost expect their relationships to go bad. They have a marked fear of closeness and a lack of trust. Avoidant individuals are more skeptical and doubtful of the existence of romantic love, and they believe that they do not need a love partner in order to be happy. Their key relationship struggles include:

1. Having a fear of closeness.

2. Having a belief that people are not trustworthy.

3. Feeling that others are not dependable.

4. Doubting that his or her relationships will last.

5. Having relationships where his or her partner wants more closeness, but he or she does not allow this to occur.

Individuals who are avoidant often show limited emotion in relationships and can be hard to read. They are uncomfortable being close to others and others find them hard to be around. Others get glimpses of their goodness but are often disappointed by their lack of consistency. They are nervous when anyone gets too near, and often love partners want them to be more intimate than they feel comfortable being.

Attachment Style 3: Anxious/Ambivalent

Individuals who fall in the anxious/ambivalent relationship style experience love as preoccupying. It is painful to watch them. Their relationships start with a burst of energy, and then their overzealous nature tends to overwhelm their partner. This creates a tense period of time where they feel jealous and fearful that the relationship will end. Their most dominant desire is to connect with another person, but they often feel like they are doing most of the work in their relationships. They typically fall in love frequently and easily but have difficulty finding true love. They also have more self-doubts than the other two types because, unlike avoidant respondents, they do not repress or attempt to hide feelings of insecurity.

Those who score high in this category often:

1. Obsess about relationships

2. Are quick to fall in love

3. Experience emotional ups and downs in relationships

4. Have a strong desire for reciprocation and union in relationships

5. Struggle with feelings of jealousy

Those who fall in the anxious/ambivalent category find that others are reluctant to get as close as they would like. They often worry that their partner doesn't really love them or won't want to stay with them. They want to merge completely with another person, and this desire sometimes scares people away.

Researchers who have spent time evaluating these different styles of relationship attachment have pinpointed interesting facts about satisfaction and longevity. Those individuals who feel secure reported that their relationships were happy, friendly, and trusting. They were able to accept and support their partners despite faults. Those in a secure relationship tended to have longer relationships and fewer divorces than individuals in the other two categories.

Individuals in avoidant attachment relationships reported many highs and lows. They often struggled with jealousy and a fear of closeness. They had a higher divorce rate than individuals who reported a secure relationship style.

Those who categorize themselves in the anxious/ambivalent category experience love as obsession, as a high desire for reciprocation and union, and as extreme sexual attraction and jealousy (Hazan & Shaver, 1987). The anxious/ambivalent individual also had a higher divorce rate than individuals who reported a secure relationship style.

Connection Style

CONNECTION STYLE 1: Secure

CONNECTION STYLE 2: Avoidant

CONNECTION STYLE 3: Anxious/Ambivalent

Attachment styles clearly impact how individuals approach connections. It is important for individuals to assess their own attachment style and that of the people they date. For example, someone who is anxious/ambivalent may have such a strong need to be "in" a relationship that they scare others away. Ironically, the very thing that they want and need the most is not happening because of their own intense desires.

To get more in depth information on relationship connection visit www. stopmarryingmistakes.com to read the special reports and take the connection quiz.

ASSIGNMENT 59A: Read each of the three relationship attachment styles above. Which statement most closely represents how you feel about relationships? Explain your answer.

ASSIGNMENT 59B: Review each of the three attachment styles of love again. Throughout the years, has your relationship style changed or has it been consistent? Explain your answer.

If you find that you're not comfortable with the category in which you find yourself, there are some things you can do. One of the most helpful things you can do is learn what a healthy attachment looks like.

Secure Relationship Characteristics

1. They are happy in relationships. For them, happiness comes from learning about and enjoying the company of others. They don't feel like they have to be in a relationship and are comfortable being by themselves.

2. They have many friends. Their friendships develop over time and last for many years.

3. Commonly, they trust others and themselves. Trust is a main component of their relationships.

4. They do not have a fear of closeness. People with secure relationship characteristics have no reservations about getting close to another person. They are able to connect emotionally with others.

5. The emotional ups and downs are limited. Emotional extremes are not very common. Their relationships are characterized by stability and peace.

6. They don't experience a lot of jealousy. Secure people choose to be with others who are reliable and trustworthy.

7. They have a desire to form a close relationship, but they don't get caught up worrying about not being in one.

As you review the characteristics of individuals who fit in the secure attachment style, identify one or two areas where you can improve. Remember, your goal is to become as healthy as possible. Your challenge is to create a safe environment around you so that people will desire to be close to you.

ASSIGNMENT 60: As you review the list of seven characteristics of secure attachment styles, which of the items are not a problem for you?

ASSIGNMENT 61: Which of the seven qualities listed above do you need to improve? Ask those who are close to you and whom you trust what they think about you. If there is no one you can ask, this is a sign that work in the area of trust may be needed. If you think that everyone is out to get you, and that there literally isn't anyone in the would who can be trusted, you might want to visit with a counselor and work through some deeper issues in order to free yourself from anxiety and fear.

What is one action step that you can take to improve your relationship style?

Dating with Confidence: Physical Safety

In order for people to date with confidence, they first need to take measures to be safe. No matter whether you are a man or woman, dating and/or thinking of marriage can pose risks. Some of the risks can be painful, with possibly even grave consequences. On the other hand, there is the chance of a beautiful, fulfilling relationship. So how does one stay safe?

4 Guidelines to Keeping Yourself Safe

1. Listen to Your Instincts

The number one way to keep yourself safe in the dating world is to stay in tune with your instincts. Nothing acts as a better guide. If something is telling you this relationship is wrong, don't talk yourself out of believing the warning because the person is spiritual, fun, good-looking, or others are talking you into it. *Listen*—no other guideline can take the place of the messages your gut gives. Some examples of red flags are:

• Your date loses his/her temper for little or no reason.

• You Feel as though you have to be careful what you say.

• Your date is secretive, never introducing you to family or friends.

• Your date is suddenly distant after being affectionate.

2. Take Time

Taking your time as you get involved in a relationship is critical. There is no other factor that can give you more information and more pieces to the puzzle than to see a person in many different environments over a long period of time. There is a belief that the best way to tell who a person really is, is to observe that person in a variety of stressful situations and watch how he or she responds. Some people are known to create these scenarios, but that is not necessary. Life has a way of bringing up problems.

Another reason to take your time getting involved is because abusers like to do the exact opposite. Perpetrators are known to be charming, charismatic, outgoing people who want to sign the deal quickly before their mask slips. A truly good person will become more evident with time

and trial, but a perpetrator can only hold up the mask so long. If anyone wants to move too quickly into exclusive dating or wants to limit time and choices with others, it sends up a red flag.

3. Make Sure You Are Ready

Many singles don't take the time to heal from their previous relationship before jumping into another. This can cause all sorts of problems. If people don't heal first, they are taking a huge risk of making the same mistake for the exact same reasons they did the first time—hurting from old childhood wounds, feeling uncomfortable with themselves, and feeling lonely.

One of the best ways to determine if you're ready to move into another relationship is to ask a close friend or family member how often you talk about your previous relationship or how focused your thoughts are on getting involved in another one. This is a benchmark or clue. If you are still talking about your past relationship several times a week, and past wounds seem to occupy your thoughts, it is not time to move on. More healing is necessary. If you aren't comfortable with yourself, and you continually think getting involved with someone else is going to magically make everything better, it's time to wait and do more personal emotional work.

4. Research

Another important step in making sure you are safe in your dating relationships is to research the people you're dating. Don't let romance blind common sense. Know that not everyone is honest. Discreetly, and if possible, check credit reports, professional licensing information with the state, and his or her background. Learn about the career of your new interest. Call his or her work and ask

> **If people don't heal first, they are taking a huge risk of making the same mistake for the exact reasons they did the first time.**

direct questions about the type of person you are considering. Ask people in the same field about how the business works so you have something on which to base the stories you're being told. Check to see if his or her home address is listed in the phone book. Take other necessary steps to determine that the person's identity is who he says he is. If the opportunity presents itself, talk to church members and your love interest's coworkers. Encourage comments and opinions from others. People are often honest when asked. These are just some of the ways you can get a better idea of who you're getting involved with. Find out as much as you can about this person's past, and be prepared to provide the same information about yourself.

Don't be afraid to ask your potential date many questions. Ask about previous relationships. If your date won't tell you, consider that a warning sign. He or she might be trying to hide something. It's also possible that he or she has not resolved his or her own past issues. If, when speaking about the past, the situation is always the ex's fault, pay attention. Work on compatibility and personality tests together to promote insightful conversation. An excellent resource for this would be *Knowing Who's Right and Avoiding Who's Wrong* by Barbara DeAngelis.

Four Guidelines to Keeping Yourself Safe

1. Listen to Your Instincts

2. Take Time

3. Make Sure You Are Ready

4. Research

Nothing will give you better insight on the quality of your dates than keeping a record of what your instincts and emotions are telling you when you are with this person over the course of time. To help you have a clear picture on what your repeated feelings and impressions are, go to www.stopmarryingmistakes.com and download the **Climate Date Tracker**.

What to do if some of these warning signs fit you.

Most people are abusive on one level or another. It's a matter of degree. If most of the negative qualifications fit you or someone you love, all is not lost. Many things can be done. One of the best things to do is to become educated, and know why you behave the way you do and what better coping tools you could learn or develop. There are many good therapists who can be helpful and many programs that are designed to be of service. Honesty with oneself precedes the ability to evaluate others.

Can You Date With Confidence?

Dr. Skinner told me: I have heard many people say, "If only I had more confidence while dating, I always seem to do something which ends up ruining my relationships." Dating with confidence is not that complicated. It does require a belief in oneself and the development of the right skills. Once these two elements are in place, every individual can date with confidence. Unfortunately, skills that make relationships last get little attention or focus in our society. Here are a few key elements for you to think about as you consider what it takes to date with confidence. Answer each item by circling the response which best describes you.

Can You Date with Confidence Quiz?

a) True or False—I believe that I can develop a deep and lasting connection.

b) True or False—I am good at creating an environment where people want to be with me.

c) True or False—When I am frustrated with the person I am dating, I am good at solving the problem.

d) True or False—I am good at communicating my concerns to another person without offending or hurting them.

e) True or False—I am a person others can love.

f) True or False—I am good at showing the people I date that I value them.

g) True or False—I don't have to hide anything from the people I date.

If you answered True to each of these questions, you can feel confident about dating. You have good skills and qualities that make relationships work. If you answered false on any, you have some work to do, but remember to take one issue at a time.

Dating and Relationship Expectations

After going through a divorce, do you think your expectations about relationships have changed? In this section, you will be asked to identify some basic expectations you have. Your expectations help you make decisions about whether to date someone or not. For example, you probably expect the people you date to be attractive to you. You may expect that the person you date will dress and act appropriately in public. You may not think of these things as expectations. They are the automatic filters that dictate whether you start dating a person and continue to date them.

Your expectations help you make decisions about whether to date someone or not.

It's important that you take time and evaluate what your specific expectations are.

ASSIGNMENT 62: Make a list of at least ten expectations that you have in your dating relationships. Once you have completed it, rank the order from most important to least.

1

2

3

4

5

6

7

8

9

10

Now that you have identified some of your expectations, it is time to consider how they are helping or hurting your relationships. A woman fully expected the man she was dating to help her pay her bills. She also wanted him to buy her new clothes each time they went to the mall. These expectations eventually pushed him away. In another case, a man thought that the woman he dated must automatically make him her most important priority. This expectation ignored the needs of his date and was destructive.

Most people also have positive expectations. Here is a short list of common expectations shared by those in successful relationships:

Successful Expectations:

1. Honesty

2. Trustworthiness

3. Open communication

4. A good job

5. Financial responsible

6. Uncritical

7. Lifts others up

8. Sense of humor

9. Availability

10. Shows others that they are important

11. Acknowledges mistakes

12. Will talk about anything

13. Good personal grooming habits

14. Supportive

15. Respects others

An acquaintance shared this story with a therapist not long after she was divorced: I was dating a man and we had been talking about our ex-spouses. During the conversation, he turned to me and asked if I still had feelings for my ex-husband. I didn't know what to say. Initially, I wanted to say no, but I knew that wasn't true so I told him I did. His response was interesting. He said, 'Had you told me that you didn't have feelings for your ex-spouse, I probably wouldn't have asked you out again. I sense your feelings for him, and had you not admitted it I would have had a hard time trusting you.'

This story illustrates the importance this man placed on honesty in relationships. Just as interesting is the fact that he was willing to tell my acquaintance what he expected. His forthright manner put my friend at ease.

I went out with a guy once who asked if I would take care of him too since I obviously had the mother thing down. His expectation of being taken care of didn't meet my expectation of getting involved in an equal partnership. With our different expectations out in the open, it became clear we weren't compatible.

It's interesting that each of us has expectations about dating and relationships, but seldom do we clearly identify them. Rarely do we discuss them with the people we date. One way that we could increase the chances of being successful in relationships is to candidly discuss these things. Many people have married without fully understanding what their spouse expected out of the relationship. In many instances, had the expectations been known, the marriage may have never taken place. For example, a man who expects three home cooked meals and his jeans ironed with a crease down the pant leg and a woman who expects to be supported in her exciting career pursuits might not be the best match. The conflicts between these two lifestyles would come to the immediate foreground if the two talked about their expectations ahead of time.

One way that we could increase the chances of being successful in relationships is to candidly discuss our expectations.

ASSIGNMENT 63: Take time and write down the expectations that your ex-spouse had and how that made your relationship more challenging.

1

2

3

4

5

ASSIGNMENT 64: List the expectations you had and how that made the relationship more challenging.

1

2

3

4

5

ASSIGNMENT 65: Make a list of expectations that you will not tolerate in a relationship.

1

2

3

4

5

Dating can be an exciting yet scary opportunity. It can also be a fantastic chance to explore and gain wisdom about yourself and others. If you take common sense precautions, and are willing to honestly work on your own issues, dating can be a great time in your life.

ASSIGNMENT 66: Make a list of expectations that you absolutely must have in order for a relationship to be successful.

1

2

3

4

5

By understanding life principles and how they operate in relationships, it's easier to maintain good relations and either turn around, or leave, bad ones. It takes a lot of honest, hard work to come from a place of being less than perfect, but the rewards are great.

REFERENCE:

Olsen, D.H., and DeFrain, J. *Marriage and the Family: Diversity and Strengths.* Mountain View, California: Mayfield Publishing, 1994.

Hazan, C. & Shaver, P. *Conceptualizing romantic love as an attachment process.* Journal of Personality and Social Psychology, 1987, 511–524.

CHAPTER 12

SECRETS ABOUT GENUINE INTIMACY

Picture this: you and your companion are traveling on a long journey through a mountain wilderness, you're seeing unique vegetation, cultures, and animals. At first, you enjoy being with this person as you journey together. The partnership brings a sense of fun, understanding, and belonging as you share your adventures.

As time progresses, tension begins to increase. You experience new frustrations, but you continue to hope that the relationship will get back to what it was. The disagreements continue, though, and turn into arguments and fights. The harder you try to fix the situation, the worse it gets.

As the environment you share with your companion becomes more hostile, you come to a fork in the road. You look at the different paths and determine that going right would be best. You step in that direction only to be tugged back. Shocked, you look at your partner who explains that you're making the wrong choice. This tugging to go opposite directions happens over and over again. Sometimes you win. Other times your partner does. But you notice as you try to move ahead together that this constant fighting slows your progress and destroys the joy you were feeling. You talk to your partner about your concerns but no real solution emerges. After months in this tug-of-war, you both decide to continue the journey separately.

Filled with hesitancy, you move alone down your chosen path. After a while, the freedom you feel quickens your pace. You walk with a lighter step because you're finally free of arguments, criticism, or general negativity. When different paths present themselves, you smile as you spring forward without encountering any resistance.

As time goes on, you see stunning landscapes, meet unique people, and have unusual experiences. This creates a gnawing desire to share your adventures with someone. You can't find anyone who knows you well enough to really stop and listen. If you do share something with a passerby, they nod, give you a confused look, and go on. This merely serves to increase your desire to be understood and share what is happening to you. One day you realize that, although it's nice to travel without resistance, it's lonely to be by yourself.

You think that maybe you should try getting another partner, but you remember your last experience. You don't know if you dare. Achieving your desire of intimacy with someone seems impossible.

You have probably already guessed that the above story reflects a common problem in relationships. People want to feel connected, understood, and yet free to be themselves. When relationships start, it seems like everything is going to be perfect, but soon it becomes clear you don't have the connection you thought. Problems and frustrations arise.

Are you lonely or frustrated in your relationship? Have you felt like you were unable to connect no matter what you tried? Have you ever wondered why some couples make it while others fall apart? Or have you tried to identify the key qualities that successful couples exhibit?

In this chapter we will explore different types of connections, and how to create a rewarding experience for both people involved.

Five Types of Intimacy

When you hear the word intimacy, do you automatically think of sex? Or do you define intimacy in relationships another way? Couples experience various types of intimacy in their relationships. Below is a list, with definitions, of different types of intimacy.

Intimacy 1: Physical

This is easily the most recognizable form of intimacy. Western media focuses almost exclusively on physical intimacy in relationships. Seldom are we shown how couples develop other types. Physical intimacy is definitely important; however, it is only one aspect of intimacy. Relationships will not be satisfying without other types of connection.

> **Physical intimacy is only one part of a relationship. Relationships will not be satisfying without other types of connection.**

Dr. Skinner explains: When couples come to my office with relationship problems, they will frequently say, "We don't have much in common." Many times these couples start their relationship with a lot of physical intimacy. The beginning of their relationship is exciting and fun, but they haven't taken the time to develop intimacy in other areas. Eventually, they sometimes realize that they cannot find common ground.

Intimacy 2: Emotional

When two people can share emotional intimacy in their relationship, they don't feel like they have to hide their feelings from each other. The couple has created a safe environment between them where they can share the most common emotions

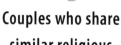

Emotional intimacy solidifies the bond of a relationship.

(enjoyment, love, sadness, shame, fear). When couples are comfortable sharing deep emotions with each other, they have developed emotional intimacy. This is often the solidifying bond in their relationship.

Emotional intimacy solidifies the bond of a relationship.

Intimacy 3: Spiritual

Couples who share similar religious beliefs and practices enjoy a rich connection.

Sharing personal beliefs in a God can have a very powerful effect on a relationship. Many people believe in a higher being. When a couple can share their thoughts and feelings on a religious nature with each other, a spiritual form of intimacy is created. Couples often do this when they pray, read religious books, attend meetings, and/or share personal experiences. (Unfortunately, some of us mistakenly believe that if we have had a spiritual experience with someone then it means we should marry them.)

Couples who share similar religious beliefs and practices enjoy a rich connection.

Intimacy 4: Psychological

Psychological trust and communication is one of the foundational elements of a healthy relationship.

This form of intimacy involves deep trust. Couples who share psychological intimacy simply know that they can trust each other. They never doubt whether personal or confidential information will be shared outside of the relationship. They also consult with one another about problems they may experience in other areas of life. They know that their partner will turn to them when in need rather than turning to someone else. This is one of the foundation stones of a healthy relationship. Psychological trust and communication is one of the foundational elements of a healthy relationship.

Intimacy 5: Cognitive

When two people share mutual interests, hobbies, and goals, they begin to share an intellectual form of intimacy.

Most people love to share their interests and hobbies with others. When it happens in a relationship, it can be even more exciting. Cognitive intimacy involves a level of thinking where two people converse deeply over a common interest. Such couples discover that they can talk for hours and hours without getting bored. Cognitive intimacy adds richness, enjoyment, and a sense of belonging to a relationship.

> **Cognitive intimacy adds richness, enjoyment, and a sense of belonging to a relationship.**

How the 5 Types of Intimacy Work in a Relationship

Not all forms of intimacy must be present for a marriage to function. The more there are the higher the relationship satisfaction. Furthermore, the types of intimacy experienced in the relationship may vary from time to time. A couple may have an intellectual discussion where both partners feel really close (cognitive intimacy), and then they may not experience that form of intimacy again for many months. However, they may have other intimate experiences connecting them emotionally and physically.

DR. SKINNER EXPLAINS: While I don't have scientific evidence to support this claim, I believe that couples need to connect in all of these areas periodically to maintain excitement and satisfaction in their relationship.

In the assignments for this section, you will be asked to identify the different types of intimacy that you have experienced in your most recent relationship (marriage or dating). As you do so, please review the definitions and explanations of each type of intimacy so that you can best evaluate your relationship(s).

How Do You Rate on The Intimacy Scale?

ASSIGNMENT 67A: Review your current or most recent relationship. What percentage of the relationship intimacy was physical, emotional, spiritual, psychological, and/or cognitive?

Physical _____%

Emotional _____%

Spiritual _____%

Psychological _____%

Cognitive _____%

Explain your percentages. If you had a high percentage on emotional, write down examples of why that worked and was good. Do this for all the high scores.

For the low scores, write down how you were different from the person with whom you were in relationship. How did that affect the outcome of your happiness together? Were you able to override it, or was it a deal breaker?

Now visualize the spots where you scored low, and picture how you would like it to be. How does it look? Feel? Write down the details of this experience.

ASSIGNMENT 67B: Do you believe that the percentages you identified above were good or bad for your relationship? Please explain.

ASSIGNMENT 67C: As you evaluate your current or previous relationship, what type(s) of intimacy kept the relationship together? What was lacking? Do you know why it was lacking?

Ask a good friend who has often observed you and your partner together to offer feedback. What does this person think worked in your relationship? Where did he or she sense something was missing?

ASSIGNMENT 67D: Look back over your important relationships. Can you identify your patterns? What are they?

Stopping the Unhealthy Connection

As you consider the different types of intimacy, what can you determine is your pattern of connection? For example, do you find that most of your relationships only have one or two kinds of intimacy? Have you had the same type of connection over and over again, or have you had different forms? As you review your previous relationships, there are hints that can help you become more aware and avoid the pitfalls the next time you become involved.

ASSIGNMENT 68: If you see patterns emerging as you study your past relationships, what steps can you take to ensure that your present or future relationships won't experience these same pitfalls?

Through examination of the different areas of intimacy, and the analyses of your strengths and weaknesses, you can now form closer, healthier connections. Careful, thoughtful selection in your future partner choices will make your journey through the dating wilderness much more enjoyable.

The Five Secrets to Intimacy

Creating a deep, lasting relationship connection is a challenge for many people. Dr. Skinner often asks class members what real intimacy looks like. In other words, what do two people do to achieve a satisfying, close relationship? If you are like most, you have never thought about the details and will draw a blank. Let's see how well you do.

ASSIGNMENT 69: What does a deeply connected relationship look like for you? What would the interplay between you and another person be?

Many of us get into a relationship with only a bit of an idea of what we want. We lack the step-by-step knowledge of what holds relationships together.

Principles are what make relationships work.

Universal principles govern whether or not relationships work. Let's look at what these are.

Intimacy Secret 1: Commitment to Integrity

A healthy relationship requires honesty with yourself and others about what you're feeling and thinking. To be successful with this, a person must stay true to doing right and good in any situation. A person must remain consistent in his or her actions, thoughts, feelings, and heart.

If someone has integrity, that person can usually be trusted. Mr. Smith, in the movie *Mr. Smith Goes to Washington*, is an excellent example. No matter what outside pressures were placed on him, he remained true to his principles.

The foundation to healthy relationships is trust, which can only be developed when both partners are completely honest.

Four Rules to Living with Integrity:

Integrity Rule 1: I am totally honest, recognizing that a lie is any communication given with the intent to deceive.

Too many people trick themselves into believing they are being honest even though they are leaving out important information in their communication. There are various reasons why someone would delete data. One of the most common reasons is to stay out of trouble. They know if the other person knew the whole truth they would be upset.

Another reason to withhold information is to avoid hurting another person's feelings. However, what harms the relationship more than telling the truth is not telling it. Keep in mind that a person should strive to use common sense in this area.

Integrity Rule 2: Unless I am released from commitments, I must keep them.

Many people have a hard time with this one. They say they will call on such and such a day and they don't, or they will be at an appointment or do this or that and it doesn't happen. This occurs so often in our society that there are cartoons and jokes poking fun at this tendency.

The excuse most people use is that other things came up, or they didn't think the commitment was serious. What these people don't understand is how much harm they create by not doing what they say they're going to do. Every time a commitment is broken, trust erodes. If this occurs too often, there won't be enough belief left in the other person to keep a relationship functional.

Before you say, "But what about …" remember the first half of the statement: "Unless I am released from commitments." This means that you can get out of the obligation. For example, you said that you would pick up your girlfriend at five. Once on the highway, you come to gridlock because of an unexpected accident. A person with integrity will call the girlfriend as soon as he can and let her know that he cannot arrive at the agreed upon time, and he will be there as soon as possible. That call may seem simple. It is small acts like that which create trust.

Integrity Rule 3: I search for truth and align with it.

This is a basic concept. People with integrity want to know what the truth is, and they actively seek it. For example, let's say someone reading this book didn't realize that it is dishonest to promise to be somewhere and then not show up. He or she doesn't understand how that act could affect someone. After reading the above section, however, this person may set a goal not to do this anymore now that they understand the impact their actions have on others. They might make mistakes trying to live up to the new standard. That's okay. The important part is that they are trying to change.

Integrity Rule 4: I willingly take responsibility for any problem I cause, and, to the extent possible, make it right.

This principle is one of those with which people often struggle. Either people like to believe that they are completely innocent of all wrongdoing, or they like to take total responsibility for every problem. Learning how to figure out what part is your mistake and what is not can be tricky. If you wrestle with this, talking with a trusted adviser over your situation can be extremely helpful.

Rules to Integrity

Rule 1

I am totally honest, recognizing that a lie is any communication given with the intent to deceive.

Rule 2

Unless I am released from commitments, I must keep them.

Rule 3

I search for truth and align with it.

Rule 4

I willingly take responsibility for any problem I cause, and, to the extent possible, make it right.

Intimacy Secret 2: Commitment to Affirming Worth and Showing Genuine Compassion

Relationships are much more likely to succeed if both partners are committed to affirming each other's worth. This is especially true during conflict.

Relationships that don't last often have high conflict, put-downs, criticism, and a negative climate.

Don't underestimate this simple principle. It's easy to read it and say, "Yeah, yeah. That makes sense," then not apply it to your life. When a couple sends love and value to each other in difficulty, research has discovered that this skill determines the health and the lasting ability of the relationship. Fights are not the deciding factor of divorce. Whether the couple sends value to each other at critical times is. Think about it and look to see how you're doing. Quickly reflect on a relationship you value. The last time you fought, how did you send value during the problem? Were you more concerned with proving to the other person that they were wrong, or did you think, "How can I show I love to him/her even though we aren't agreeing?" Did you voice your validations? Did you put the other person down? Did you sneer or give angry looks? On a 1–10 scale, with ten being the highest, how would you rate yourself? If you are really brave, and truly want to know how you're doing in this area, ask the other person how you did in your last fight. Have this person give a number to you on the 1–10 scale then talk about it. Have your companion tell you how he or she felt with your behavior in the fight.

One of *the* most important skills to master in relationships is affirming worth and sending value. If this is not present, the relationship will not be satisfying or successful in the long run.

One of the hardest and most important times to affirm worth and show genuine compassion is in the face of inappropriate behavior. Yes, that means no matter what the other person is doing you let them know that they are of worth. It is important to affirm your own worth also. Take all steps necessary to ensure your safety, especially if your physical or mental well-being is at risk.

Four Principles of Affirming Worth and Showing Genuine Compassion

Affirming Worth Principle 1: All persons, including self, are of infinite worth.

When in a relationship, everyone in it needs to be treated and looked upon as having worth. People who feel their infinite worth don't allow themselves to get physically and emotionally hurt repeatedly. They see themselves as having value and not deserving of such poor treatment. They will take necessary steps to make the situation safe, or they will remove themselves from the poor treatment.

A person who sees others as having infinite worth will not treat anyone as though they have little or no value. To live the principle of affirming worth, you should take all steps necessary to make sure others are treated with respect. If others are being mistreated, you would want to take steps to help that individual.

Affirming Worth Principle 2: Behavior, for the most part, is learned.

People behave the way they do because at some point in their lives they were taught to behave that way, either at home, at school, or on the street. Experiences shape us all.

Affirming Worth Principle 3: Misbehavior is almost always the symptom of some other problem.

This goes right back to beliefs. When someone acts out, the root cause will be something less apparent than what it seems. For example, the Humane Society was notified that there was a dog apparently starving to death in someone's backyard. When they investigated, they found a German Shorthair that weighed only forty pounds. Every rib could be counted. The dog could not lift its head, much less bark. When the owner was charged with animal cruelty and went to court, he admitted that he deliberately tried to starve the dog to death. Such cruelty is not innate in human beings. It was later discovered that this man had grown up in an abusive home where he was often forced to go hungry, not only for food, but also any human contact or affection.

Another example of how acting out is caused by a belief was seen when I started cooking dinner one night. I had just turned on the gas on the stove when my six-year-old boy suddenly ran out of the room, then the house, screaming. He was shaking, refusing to come back in. It took weeks of me working with him to find out what the cause of his behavior was. It turned out that the firemen came to school earlier that day telling him about the dangers of fire. My boy had developed a belief that if he saw a flame he would die. It took a lot of work to dispel this belief.

Affirming Worth Principle 4: Behavior is belief-linked.

Most poor behavior is the direct result of a belief. The belief could be, "The whole world is out to get me and I must defend myself at all costs." A person with this belief will become defensive and will not see any of the good that might be hidden in a situation.

When you are a parent or an authority figure, one of your greatest efforts should be to help children change these destructive beliefs. When children no longer believe the world is out to wreak vengeance and that their parents love them and want to protect them, their behavior will reflect their new beliefs.

4 Principles to Affirming Worth and Showing Genuine Compassion

Principle 1

All persons, including self, are of infinite worth.

Principle 2

Behavior, for the most part, is learned.

Principle 3

Misbehavior is almost always the symptom of some other problem.

Principle 4

Behavior is belief-linked.

Intimacy Secret 3: Commitment to Growth

In every partnership, it is important to be committed to growth. When couples want to cultivate their bond, they share their deepest thoughts and feelings with each other. Successful partners do this in ways that enrich their connection. Many happy couples form rituals that help cement their relationship (i.e., phone calls during the day, notes left on the car, a gift that is given out of the blue, a goodnight kiss,).

Five Principles to Growth

There are five growth principles that ensure a relationship is a healthy, fun connection. If there are snags in your relationship, study the following concepts carefully and figure out what areas need improvement.

Commitment to Growth Principle 1: A temporary steward teaches, trains, motivates, places protective barriers, and requires accountability.

The first principle has to do with relationships where there is an adult/child situation such as parent/child or teacher/student. Under these situations, the governing person should create barriers by which the younger child/student should live. A parent would be failing in their job if they allowed their child to run in front of a moving car, based on the reasoning that they were allowing the child to grow and didn't want to hurt their freedom to choose.

The temporary steward does a balancing act, keeping an eye on what the person they are protecting can handle and what they cannot. They will put protective barriers around the child until the child has mastered the skill. They will also teach the child the skills they need to be able to branch out on their own. This process also includes inspiring the child to believe they can do it.

An example of this is seen when a parent tries to teach a five year old how to tie his or her shoes. The protective barrier that many parents undertake before their child reaches four or five is to buy their child Velcro shoes so their child doesn't trip over the shoe laces (protective barrier). Depending on the child and the parent, when the parent judges the child is capable, he or she will begin instructing the child how to make the famous bunny ears out of the shoe lace (training). The parent will often tell the child that they can do it and they want to see them try (motivates). When the child masters the skill of tying his or her shoes, the parent will let the child tie his or her shoes from then on (letting go of stewardship).

> **Relationships go out of whack when people in the relationship try to be a temporary steward of their spouse or their dating partner.**

Relationships go out of whack when one or more of the people in the relationship try to be a temporary steward of their spouse dating partner. This is seen when one or the other acts like the parent or child. Be on guard for this. Being a temporary steward over your child or your student at school is appropriate, but being the mommy or daddy in a partnership is not healthy.

Commitment to Growth Principle 2: It is a basic human desire to make our own decisions.

Face it, after we move away from our parents, we don't search for someone who will tell us what to do for the rest of our lives. Wait a minute. Think about this. Do we? Most people don't intentionally look for someone they can boss around or for someone to boss them around. This sort of imbalance happens often even though it goes against our need to feel that we are making our own decisions. When the people involved in a relationship don't allow choice to occur for both parties, the relationship is not healthy and needs adjusting.

Commitment to Growth Principle 3: Everyone has the seeds for solutions to their own problems within themselves.

MOST PEOPLE THINK: when I get rich, when I have kids, when the kids leave, when I meet the perfect partner, when I get married, when I get divorced, my problems will be solved. This is simply not the truth. No matter what happens and no matter where you go, you will be stuck with yourself.

I've tried to escape myself before. I couldn't do it, and you can't either. I was guilty of the Romeo myth, believing that someone would sweep into my life and fix my problems. They would love me, adore me, and know how to handle every situation that came up. I waited and waited and waited until one day I got tired of all the waiting because some really sticky situations were occurring. As I waited, these situations did nothing but expand. So I started doing the work and fixing the problems until Prince Charming could arrive on the scene.

Romeo has never come, and now I am married. Truthfully, there are a lot of great things about Doug, but he doesn't solve all my problems. He doesn't take away all my fear and frustrations, and sometimes he even creates frustrations. That's right, I married a normal male. No Prince Charming for me, and I doubt anyone else has found one either. In the case of males, no Stepford wife exists. Sorry. (Not really.)

Commitment to Growth Principle 4: Self-esteem rises in direct proportion to the amount of responsibility a person takes for his or her own actions.

Do you feel blue? Is your self-esteem shot from divorce? Do you wonder if you will ever feel good about yourself again? Here's the formula to regaining that good feeling—take responsibility for your life, your situation, your choices, your behavior. You are the one who chose to marry who you did, and you were the one who signed

> **The formula to regain that good feeling again— take responsibility for your life, your situation, your choices, and your behavior.**

the divorce papers. It's important for your mental well-being to take responsibility for the part you played that got you into your present situation. If you don't like it, change it. You are in charge of your life. Blaming others will cause you to lose friends, and your self-esteem will take a dive.

The formula to regain that good feeling again— take responsibility for your life, your situation, your choices, and your behavior.

Commitment to Growth Principle 5: Skillful stewards sustain those under them or in their charge.

It's difficult in the dating world to tell a person of character and caliber from a person who is a great actor. One of the ways to detect on which side people fall is to study how they treat those under their authority. This could mean employees, children, or even parents and grandparents, if they're ailing. The trick is to notice the details. Is your love interest bossy and edgy with others? Do the people under your love interest's authority want to be around him or her and say nice things behind his or her back? Do you sense tension in the air when the steward and those beneath him or her are together? How loving and flowing does the relationship seem? These are important questions to ask yourself as you observe the various situations in which you find yourself with your new spark. It also wouldn't be a bad idea to privately interview the people in your love interest's charge, if possible. (Remember that there is the possibility that if they're afraid of him or her, they won't tell the truth.)

Test: Caliber or Fraud

How does your love interest treat those who are under his or her authority?

5 Principles to Commitment to Growth

Principle 1

A temporary steward teaches trains, motivates, places protective barriers, and requires accountability.

Principle 2

Men's/Women's basic drive is to make their own decisions.

Principle 3

Everyone has the seeds for solutions to their own problems within themselves.

Principle 4

Self-esteem rises in direct proportion to the amount of responsibility a person takes for his or her own actions.

Principle 5

Skillful stewards sustain those under them or in their charge.

> *Intimacy Secret 4: Commitment to Agency: The Key to Becoming a Self-Governing, Course-Correcting Individual*

In relationships, individuals should feel free to be themselves. In a relationship without freedom of choice, one partner might feel forced to share what they are feeling and thinking. In addition, agency doesn't exist if one person is telling another what he or she should be feeling and thinking. Even if one person disagrees with how someone else is feeling, to tell him or her that those feelings are wrong is a violation of the principle of agency. In a relationship where agency exists, both people feel that they can share their thoughts, feelings, and emotions with each other.

There are four principles which will make this concept clearer.

Agency Principle 1: People are not totally free or moral agents unless they are taught the principles, truths, laws, rules, policies, and procedures that can impact them.

If you don't understand the principles or concept behind an action, you can't be totally free. Let's take, for instance, the child who was taught that he could have anything he wanted. If he went into a grocery store, took a candy bar, and tried to leave the store without paying, he could get caught and sent to jail.

This child didn't have agency for his choice because he didn't know that stealing was against the law, and that by taking the candy bar he risked going to jail. If a person is taught that they can have anything they want if they work and pay for it, they will have the agency to make decisions concerning their behavior.

> **If we don't take the time to learn how human behavior works and how the interactions affect others, our agency will be limited.**

This same concept works in relationships. If you don't take the time to learn how human behavior works and how interactions affect each of us, your agency will be limited and you may be choosing outcomes that you would rather not have out of ignorance.

If we don't take the time to learn how human behavior works and how the interactions affect others, our agency will be limited.

Agency Principle 2: We must understand the positive consequences for adhering to principles and the negative consequences for violating them.

Until a person fully comprehends what they are choosing, their agency is hindered. Great care needs to go into understanding what you're getting into and what you're choosing. If you don't, you are limiting your own choices through laziness. The lack of understanding how principles work in a relationship can lead to unpleasant results.

Agency Principle 3: We must be prepared to meet opposition from those who seek to manipulate our behavior in order to control us.

In a perfect world, we would be able to make choices about our life and what we want to do without anyone going against our decisions. Unfortunately, it isn't a perfect world, and people do seek to manipulate. They often have many motives. More often than not, those that do manipulate others mean to harm the person they are trying to control. This being the case, wise individuals prepare themselves to withstand attacks of manipulation and control. Self-esteem is a big component in this endeavor. Building up your sense of self will help protect you from those who would attempt to manipulate you.

Taking care to know who you are and what you want is very important before you start interfacing in the dating world. Furthermore, trust your instincts, honor and know them, and have appropriate tools planned out in advance, such as a set of guidelines stating what you will do to help others and what you won't, before you deal with dominating family members, neighbors, and friends.

Agency Principle 4: We all must have unfettered choice.

If you're going to live your life by adhering to principles, you will grant not only yourself but also those around you the freedom to make their own choices. This doesn't mean that you don't speak up for yourself. It does mean that after you voice your concerns, you must then let others make their own decisions.

This can be an extremely difficult thing to do, especially when human emotions are involved. This might require letting someone you love walk away from you. It might require allowing someone to make decisions that you know will hurt him or her. This might require sacrifices on many different levels. Being a person of character makes it worthwhile. In the long run, it's best to grant people freedom of choice, even if you think what they are doing is wrong.

4 Principles to Commitment to Agency

Principle 1

People are not totally free or moral agents unless they are taught the principles, truths, laws, rules, policies, and procedures, that can impact them.

Principle 2

We must understand the positive consequences for adhering to principles and the negative consequences for violating them.

Principle 3

We must be prepared to meet opposition from those who seek to manipulate our behavior in order to control us.

Principle 4

We all must have unfettered choice.

> *Intimacy Secret 5: Commitment to Trusting Your Instincts Or Your Own Intuitive Responses*

In every relationship it's critical to trust your instincts in order to help you solve problems. Dr. Skinner shared the following with me: In many cases, clients have told me that when they look within themselves, they know how to respond and what to say. Their instincts help them solve problems. Your instincts are guides that can help you know who you should avoid.

Let's look at three more subset principles which go along with trusting your instincts.

Trust Your Instincts 1: We are emotional beings with an innate capacity to sense, to feel, to detect, and to discern emotions from any source. Emotion is our first language.

Have you ever felt really uneasy with someone? Have you ever felt like a business deal was bad, even though logically it seemed good? Have you ever felt like you shouldn't marry a certain individual? These are your instincts working. They detect and discern things of which our conscious minds aren't aware. Much trouble and stress can be avoided by listening to our instincts and respecting what they tell us.

Emotions were the first language we responded to in infancy. Sometimes we still respond without knowing what we're doing. Taking time to listen to our feelings will give us added depth and insight into our circumstances. It's also a rewarding endeavor because it makes us slow down and pay attention to how we are feeling and what is truly going on.

Trust Your Instincts Principle 2: Emotions are neither good nor bad. They are natural alarms.

They are keys to understanding what has happened or is happening to us. They alert us to external encroachments.

Emotions are our friends. If we feel uneasy about something, it doesn't necessarily mean not to do it. It does mean the signal should be examined to determine what exactly is making you feel uncomfortable.

When I start feeling uneasy I know I need to pay attention to what is happening to me both externally and internally. To determine whether the uneasiness comes from your issues and emotions or from your inner wisdom there are some guidelines. If it's your internal guidance system, a certain peace comes along with the feeling. If it's your issues, the impressions will change with different times of day or different thoughts.

> *Trust Your Instincts Principle 3: One who sharpens his skills in discerning, focusing on, and responding to the intimations of the heart opens the doorway to profound learning experiences.*

Once I understood how to turn inward to my conscience, or higher power or whatever you want to call it, for answers, my path opened to understanding not only more about myself but also more about the people around me and my environment. I have learned what makes me uncomfortable and why. I have also learned to follow the impressions that bring peace. When I follow the decisions that give me a deep sense of peace, my world becomes much richer.

Commitment to Trust My Instincts and My Intuitive Responses

Principle 1

We are emotional beings first, with an innate capacity to sense, to feel, to detect, and to discern emotions from any source. Emotion is our first language.

Principle 2

Emotions are neither good nor bad. They are natural alarms. They are keys to understanding what has happened or is happening to us. They alert us to external encroachments.

Principle 3

One who sharpens his skills in discerning, focusing on, and responding to the intimations of the heart, opens the doorway to profound learning experiences.

As you review each of these principles, consider them as the foundation stones of every relationship. For example, have you ever ignored the behavior of someone who has lied to you? Or have you felt like you couldn't do or say what you wanted to because you might offend the person you were dating? Or maybe you have had an experience where someone tried to convince you that what you were thinking or feeling was wrong. The point is this: If you want to develop a healthy relationship, incorporate principles 1) intimacy 2) affirming worth 3) commitment to growth 4) agency, and 5) trust your instincts. Then, evaluate how the people you date treat you by using these five principles as a measuring stick.

Questions you might ask yourself include:

- Are we being honest with each other?

- How do we send value to each other? Do I send value to my love interest, or are other things more important to me?

- Is the person I'm dating committed to the growth of our relationship? How committed am I?

- Do I feel free to be myself in this relationship? Do I allow my partner to be free?

- What are my instincts telling me about this relationship? Does the person I'm dating value my thoughts and impressions? Do I value the other person's thoughts and impressions? Or do I wish that they wouldn't talk so much?

As you use these principles as a measuring stick, you'll find that you'll be much less likely to get involved in an abusive relationship. In addition, when you find someone who is good at applying all five of these principles, you have found a person with whom a relationship will be healthy and successful.

ASSIGNMENT 70: Review the five principles listed above and identify whether they have or have not been a part of your current or most recent relationship.

ASSIGNMENT 71: How effective are you at using these five principles in your relationships? List each principle and evaluate whether it is a strength or an area in which you need to improve.

6 Characteristics of a Healthy Relationship

What keeps couples and families together?

Dr. John DeFrain, a professor at the University of Nebraska–Lincoln, has been conducting research to determine what keeps families together and strong. He has conducted research in many countries and found that regardless of where he does his research, strong families have common behaviors that keep them together. Initially, he thought that each country or culture would have different strengths. However, the more he traveled, the more similarities he found in strong families.

Successful Relationship Quality 1: Commitment

This includes trust, honesty, dependability, and faithfulness. Relationships work best if there is a strong commitment from both parties to make it work. It becomes a lot harder to be successful when one person has more of the commitment.

Happy couples enjoy being together.

Successful Relationship Quality 2: Time Together

Couples spend quality time together and share activities, feelings, and ideas. They enjoy each other's company. Happy couples enjoy being together.

Successful Relationship Quality 3: Positive Communication

This quality includes open, straightforward discussions, cooperation rather than competition, and feelings that are shared with each other. Couples need to be partners, not competitors. Adopting the "us against them" attitude can forge a deep bond.

Successful Relationship Quality 4: Appreciation and Affection

Appreciation and affection include kindness, caring for each other, respect for individuality, and a feeling of security.

Successful Relationship Quality 5: Coping with Stress and Crisis

This refers to the couple accessing both their personal and family resources in order to help solve problems, helping each other, seeing emergencies as challenges rather than denying them, and growing together through the trial.

Successful Relationship Quality 6: Spiritual Well-Being

This relationship quality includes happiness, optimism, hope, faith, a set of shared ethical values, and a sense of peace that guides family members through life's problems. Looking at this list offers good news. Strong couples and families are not doing things that are impossible to achieve.

Granted, applying these qualities for the most part is not as easy as it sounds. Improvement can be accomplished through simple acts. Even if you're not in a relationship now, you can still work on these skills by practicing your interactions with others. When you do get involved with someone, chances are it will be a deep, meaningful relationship.

Successful Relationship Qualities

QUALITY 1: Commitment

QUALITY 2: Time Together

QUALITY 3: Positive Communication

QUALITY 4: Appreciation and Affection

QUALITY 5: Coping with Stress and Crisis

QUALITY 6: Spiritual Well-Being

ASSIGNMENT 72: When you think about your current or most recent relationship, how many of these characteristics were part of it? Which things on the list above were strengths? Which areas were missing?

ASSIGNMENT 73: Of the qualities listed above, which ones do you need to improve upon? What will you do to improve your skills in these areas?

In this chapter we learned about the five different types of intimacy and how they function in a relationship. We also explored the five secrets to intimacy and how they play a crucial role in whether a relationship is healthy or heading for trouble. Lastly, we learned about the different characteristics of a healthy relationship so we could make a comparison to our own.

In the next chapter we will look at how to avoid a difficult remarriage. There are some common pitfalls into which people slip. Once you become aware of the more familiar ones, you'll be prepared to avoid repeating the same mistakes.

CHAPTER 13

HOW TO AVOID THE PITFALLS OF A DIFFICULT REMARRIAGE

Will I Ever Marry Again?

Did your ex-spouse tell you that you wouldn't ever get married again? Perhaps your ex said you were too fat, too dumb, too ugly, or too much of a loser. In my case, I was told I had too many kids, and no one would want me because of that.

When our ex-spouses tell us things like this, we can choose whether or not to believe them. I believed my ex-husband. After all, I had six small children. Who would want to take us on? I was too old, had too much responsibility, and had too few single people out there that were my age.

My current husband's former spouse told him that he was so weird that she would like to meet the person that he would marry because she didn't think he could find a new wife. This of course haunted him. Most divorced people have memories of damaging things that were said to them, and in many cases they wonder if maybe the statements were true.

Regardless of what your previous marriage was like or what predictions of doom were laid upon you, you are more likely to remarry than someone who has never been married (U.S. National Center for Health Statistics, 1991). In fact, seventy-five to eighty percent of divorcees do remarry (Wallerstein and Blakeslee, 1989).

Unfortunately, for reasons that will be discussed below, sixty to sixty-five percent of remarriages end in divorce.

Journey into the Dark World

I found parts of the Land of Singledom shocking. Parts were good, but a lot was scary. I found the rapid fire marriage proposals which streamed in disturbing. My first offer came when I had been divorced less than a month; I had just met him a few weeks before. As the question continued to get popped, the more I understood how many of us aren't thinking about what we're doing. We're so focused and worried about marriage that we forget to use reason and common sense.

I ran into others who wouldn't consider remarriage. Some were too frightened to make any commitment, and so they avoided the issue with more vigilance than they would the plague.

I realized that my former spouse was oh-so-very wrong. I also found that there are a lot of singles who want to get married. They don't always think much about what kind of commitment they're offering. I could not entertain several proposals I received because the people asking lacked any understanding of *six kids*. We talked, we laughed, and for them, that was good enough. I didn't want to expose my children to most of my dates. Most of the askers did not have the abilities or skills needed to handle children. Like it or not, my children were the biggest and most important part of the whole package. A lot of men actually wanted to side step that area of my life. I was committed to not remarrying unless I could find a person that I was not only compatible with but who also was compatible with my children and had the same kind of parenting philosophy I maintained. I found it truly scary how so many people were not considering the magnitude of their decisions.

Seven Pitfalls of Remarriage

Professionals who research stepfamilies have identified a list of reasons why remarriages fail. Learning how to avoid the problems commonly associated with remarriage will largely depend on how you approach them.

Pitfall 1: Stepparenting

Children are the number one reason why remarriages don't last. Children often sabotage their parent's new marriage. Children have many reasons for doing this. Here is a partial list:

a. Dislike for the new stepparent.

b. Erosion of hope that their natural parents will get back together.

c. Realization that there is power in pitting one parent against the other.

d. Jealousy of the new stepparent.

e. Dislike of being parented by a stranger.

d. Need for attention.

Fights over how to parent the children can lead to many embittered feelings.

Couples encounter problems when the physical parent won't allow discipline to occur at all, or when stepparents insist on taking on the parenting role too soon. Other potentially hostile problems can occur when there is a blending of two sets of children. Favoritism can have a caustic underlying effect on the whole family structure.

Pitfall 2: Restructuring Power and Hierarchy

When a divorce occurs, there is a restructuring of the power in a family. In many instances, children will be given extra responsibility simply because a single parent cannot accomplish all the ordinary tasks alone. In other instances, one parent will attempt to take away any power or influence his or her ex-spouse has on the children. This parent will tell the children that they don't have to obey their other parent, or the parent will undermine any authority the other parent tries to use in discipline.

Even if this doesn't happen, there's the challenge of a new person coming into the family. Everyone has to figure out and accept the role of this new person. The struggle, power, and reconstruction of the operation of the family can lead to many conflicts.

Pitfall 3: Finances

Alimony and child support often create problems in new marriages. The merging of finances is not easy. Often there is no clear division from the first marriage. In addition, some couples have a hard time balancing their children's needs, especially if both spouses bring children into the marriage. Treating each child the same is challenging, especially if the ex-spouse insists that his or her child support only pays for his or her child's needs.

Pitfall 4: Unresolved Issues

Divorce forces us to reevaluate ourselves. Many people who have been divorced struggle to understand what happened. Whether the divorce was something that suddenly took place or went for months, even years, the frustration, anger, and rejection are feelings that must be explored and put to rest. Unresolved issues often lead to projection (a person is blamed for the mistakes of another), which can destroy new relationships. Some individuals will see their new spouse do something that reminds them of a behavior that their ex-spouse did, and it will trigger a reaction sequence. This trigger may cause the person to put up a wall or get upset. Ironically, the new spouse will have no idea what they've done wrong, they will only know that their new partner is acting strangely and often with hostility.

Pitfall 5: Mental Health

In most circumstances, divorce lowers a person's mental health. Depression and anxiety are often associated. Due to divorce, some individuals become so angry that they cannot let go of the pain their ex-spouse caused them. This places a lot of pressure on the human mind. The mind becomes agitated. Unfortunately, the brain can lock onto the anger, fear, or anxiety and can become addicted to the chemicals released into the system every time a negative memory or image runs through their thoughts. If this pattern remains uninterrupted, the body can form a physical addiction to anger, fear, and/or anxiety.

There are also people who become so anxious about relationship failure that they sabotage new relationships. Anxiety and fear make them incapable of letting others into their life. These individuals may have relationships, but they never deepen because they don't dare let someone fully know them. It's as though they have a tight grip on a cat that is trying to twist free of the stranglehold. In the case of people, the more the other person tries to be free, the tighter the grip becomes. Eventually the cat or person will flee. This only adds fuel to the fire of the already anxiety-ridden person, reinforcing the belief that everyone will leave them.

Pitfall 6: Fear of Intimacy

Divorce often creates a fear of intimacy. This fear stems from the negative psychological impact felt from the previous marriage. Taking a chance on another person requires tremendous risk. Many refuse to take it, thus they enter relationships unwilling to make the emotional sacrifice it takes to connect with another human being. Others who take the risk will do so cautiously, holding back, like dipping a toe into the swimming pool to see what the temperature is and not quite sure if they want to risk a full submersion. Many of these people will get into the relationship slowly and see how painful it can be. At the first sign of pain or rejection, they take their toe out of the swimming pool and go back to the emotional desert where they felt safe.

Pitfall 7: Poor Mate Selection

Many think that people who have been divorced should be good at choosing a mate. After all, if you have been divorced, you should have a clear idea of what you do and don't want in a spouse, right? Wrong! In many instances, divorced people are prone to poor mate selection. Why? There are many reasons:

a. Loneliness

b. Hurried marriage

c. Incompatibility

d. Mental instability (self, other person, or both)

e. Too many unresolved issues from a previous marriage

f. Lack of self-esteem

g. Feeling as though they need a parent for their kids

h. Financial troubles

i. A need for the societal acceptance of being married

j. Fear of being alone

k. Fear of getting to know themselves

7 Pitfalls of Remarriage

PITFALL 1: Restructuring power and hierarchy

PITFALL 2: Stepparenting

PITFALL 3: Finances

PITFALL 4: Unresolved issues

PITFALL 5: Mental health

PITFALL 6: Fear of intimacy

PITFALL 7: Poor mate selection

To keep the pitfalls of remarriage present in your mind in order to rise above them, go to www.stopmarryingmistakes.com and download the **7 Pitfalls of Remarriage Chart**.

ASSIGNMENT 74: Review the list of why remarriages fail. Which of these issues concerns you the most? What could you do to prevent this issue from hurting a new marriage? You may want to take time and evaluate each issue.

Four Rules to Making Remarriages Last

Lasting Remarriage Rule 1: Take Time to Heal Before Getting Into New Relationships

A lot of people want to hurry and get married again when they find themselves single. At least twenty-five percent of all remarriages occur within one year of the divorce (Spanier and Thompson, 1987). What people fail to take into account is that their divorces probably impacted the beliefs they formed about themselves and their interactions with others. As a result, less time can be taken to develop the new relationship. Sometimes the new spouse will become fed up with all the unresolved problems. This can cause jealousy and frustration, which can lead to marital conflict. Furthermore, during the first few months of a new marriage, the couple develops habits and patterns that govern their future. Some remarriages never recover from months or years spent fighting over an ex-spouse. Other remarriages fail because the children weren't given time to adapt. Their reactions can cause high conflict between the newly formed couple.

Lasting Remarriage Rule 2: Develop a Relationship with Stepchildren

If you're going to succeed in a remarriage where stepchildren are present, developing a relationship with the children before the marriage will go a long way toward accomplishing your goal. Since children are clearly the biggest reason for remarriage failures, it is imperative that children are incorporated into the new relationship before any marriage takes place. Children often resent stepparents. This is especially true when the stepparent is thrust abruptly into their lives. They can resent the fact that their biological parent is spending more and more time with his or her new spouse. However, when children are a part of the dating process, trust can be developed. When the new stepparent has the sanction of the children (regardless of the child's age), the new marriage has a much better chance of surviving.

Dr. Skinner shared some of his own personal experiences with me: I remember as a boy the countless hours that my stepfather spent with me playing ping-pong, football, basketball, and baseball before he married my mom. He clearly had my trust and friendship. I wanted him to marry my mom because he took the time to make me feel that he cared about me. This feeling of care and acceptance deepened throughout my childhood.

On the other hand, one needs to be cautious. When I decided that I wanted to marry my current husband, Doug, I had rarely let him spend time with my children. I learned from past mistakes that children develop bonds with those you date. It can be a traumatic experience for them to build a bond then watch it end. During those times that Doug spent with my kids, I watched the interaction carefully. Like most young children, when my kids saw a strong man they began climbing all over him, wanting horsy rides and other rollicking games. I did not step in and save the new fresh meat. Instead, I sat back and watched how he handled it. When I would meet him for a lunch date, I had my youngest, a three-year-old, with me. The child would be tired because it was naptime. I'd encourage my baby to sit by Doug, which he did. My son would immediately begin the "I'm too tired" climbing all over my date, whining.

I am not a mean mother. I wanted to see how Doug would handle things. I wanted to know what he would do when the kids were tired and hungry. I wanted to know what he would do when they wanted to play. I watched very carefully. I didn't have to encourage the kids to provoke him—they did that naturally.

As we grew serious and knew we wanted to wed, I had Doug over often. It was time for the kids to get to know him and love him. We had decided that we weren't going to do the official marriage thing until the kids came up with the idea on their own. Lucky for me and the kids, Doug loves children and loves playing with them. My children quickly recognized that it was a lot more fun when Doug was around.

It was only a matter of days with Doug hanging around and helping with the household work before my children came up with a plan. "We have an idea," they said. "How about you two get married?"

We looked embarrassed and said, "Why would you want us to do that?"

All but two said they wanted us to get married. Some of the kids even took Doug aside and told him to ask me. Eventually one afternoon, when I was driving all the kids to an appointment and Doug wasn't in the car, my seven-year-old cleared her throat. "Everyone, I have an announcement to make. I'm okay with Doug and Mom getting married."

My twelve-year-old screamed, "Noooo," and tried to talk her out of her decision, but the seven-year-old had her mind set. By that point, we had five out of six votes. My twelve-year-old wasn't happy with anything that I did, so I figured that approval rate was as good as it was going to get. We announced the upcoming wedding. We included the children in the decisions as much as possible because we figured the wedding was as much for them as it was for us. Several of them have asked that we get married again because they had a lot of fun. I can only imagine how horrible the event would have been if we hadn't taken the time to get their approval. That would have dramatically increased the difficulties of an already challenged merger.

Lasting Remarriage Rule 3: Understand the Financial Obligations of Your New Spouse

Money is an ordeal for most couples. However, finances with remarried couples present extra problems, primarily because divorced pairs often have a hard time disentangling their finances from ex-spouses. In addition, alimony and child support are two of the areas where divorced couples' finances cause challenges.

A therapist shared: I have heard countless stories from men and women who complain about the new spouse's financial struggles with the ex. Some of the most common problems include late child support payments, medical bills, business asset division, the selling of the home or other assets, and hidden money.

> **Before remarrying, it is absolutely essential that you and your new partner discuss finances.**

Since divorce is often linked to financial problems, many divorced people end up going through bankruptcy. This, too, can cause resentment in the new relationship because of bad credit and (sometimes) outstanding financial obligations.

Before remarrying, it is absolutely essential that you and your new partner discuss finances. Being completely open and honest about debt, spending habits, alimony, and child support payments will help you. If you understand each other's finances and know what you're getting into before you get married, you are much more likely to foster a team approach. You can be creative in your solutions.

Financial Obligation Questionnaire

a. Do you have financial obligations to your ex-spouse such as alimony or child-support? If so, for how long?

b. Do you have debt? If so, how much? Do you have a plan for how to pay it off?

c. Will the two of you merge your assets or keep them separate? This issue has prevented many couples from marrying. A problem can occur when one spouse has many assets from a previous marriage and the new partner has very little. In situations like this, many individuals insist that a prenuptial agreement be in place prior to the marriage. Some people become upset about the concept of a prenuptial agreement, but when it comes to remarriages, it can be one of the smartest things any of us can do. It isn't that we're planning for the failure of the marriage, it's that even before commitment to marriage, we continue to have obligations to our children. Necessary measures need to be taken to protect children and their financial well being. Funds that one party possessed before the remarriage need to remain available for the children in the event of another divorce.

d. Who will pay what bills?

Lasting Remarriage Rule 4: Establish a Cohesive Relationship

Remarriages are much more likely to succeed when the two families are able to mesh and when each individual feels like an important part of the new family. Cohesion is a sense of unity, a feeling of closeness with other family members, and a feeling of pride in belonging to or being a part of the family (Pasley and Ihinger-Tallman, 1987). As you evaluate the cohesiveness or lack of it in a relationship, you will soon realize that cohesive relationships have a stable and calming climate, whereas an incohesive climate will be stressful due to tension between family members. In situations where incohesiveness is common, many people question whether they married the right person.

Lasting Remarriage Rule 1:

Take Time to Heal Before Getting Into New Relationships

Lasting Remarriage Rule 2:

Develop a relationship with stepchildren

Lasting Remarriage Rule 3:

Understand the Financial Obligations of Your New Spouse

Lasting Remarriage Rule 4:

Establish a Cohesive Relationship

Go to www.stopmarryingmistakes.com to download your own decorative copy of the **4 Rules of Making Remarriage Last.**

Preparing Children for Remarriage

Preparing children for remarriage is seldom easy. Researchers have consistently found that children are the number one reason for second marriage divorces. This does not mean that children cause the divorce, but rather their presence makes remarriages more difficult to maintain and sustain.

Researchers have consistently found that children are the number one reason for second marriage divorces.

Reduce Casualties

While children are the number one cause of failed remarriages, there are ways to reduce the casualties. Many divorced people assume that because they love someone then their children will automatically like that person as well. There are also those who leave their children completely out of the decision making process. This is one of the biggest mistakes that can occur in remarriages. Below you will find a few ideas on how to appropriately set the stage to help your children adjust to the idea of a new marriage.

Setting the Stage

SETTING THE STAGE 1: Never hide the relationship from your children.

SETTING THE STAGE 2: As your relationship progresses, involve your children in activities. You should always observe how your dating partner interacts with your children. You should be having many real life experiences to see how your partner responds. This should go on for a long time. Those who plan to manipulate or abuse you would find it very difficult to keep up his or her mask for an extended period of time.

SETTING THE STAGE 3: Take your time. Many remarriages occur so fast that the building of the relationship bond between the child and the stepparent doesn't have time to develop. Consequently, the child doesn't trust the stepparent. The results of this can be disastrous.

> Children need to build a relationship of trust and friendship with the new parent.

Children need to build a relationship of trust and friendship with the new parent.

SETTING THE STAGE 4: As the relationship turns toward marriage, discuss this possibility with the child. Be open and frank. Solicit your child's opinions. Don't feel like you have to defend the person you're dating because this can shut your child down. Listen to your child's concerns without being judgmental. If you disagree, you can tell the child that you will pay attention to his or her concerns. You may also ask your child to look at his or her own assumptions and evaluate them. In other words, you are not reaching any conclusions. You both are going to be gathering more information. If you override your child's concerns, you may find that your child will resent you and your new spouse. This resentment seldom disappears.

SETTING THE STAGE 5: Never demand that your child has to like your dating partner. Let your child slowly engage in the relationship. Some children will automatically resent the people you date because they want you to get back with your ex. Give children a lot of flexibility as they warm to the idea of you dating again. If they don't appear to ever be warming up, you may want to have a one-on-one with your child to discuss your observations. In this circumstance, you are simply trying to understand your child's concerns. Preaching or telling your child how he or she should feel is inappropriate. If your child is being rude or inconsiderate, you will want to ask your child why and establish a proper boundary. If you struggle with this delicate balance, seek professional help.

SETTING THE STAGE 6: Avoid making negative comparisons between the person you're dating and your ex-spouse. Let your child make his or her own observations. Many children love the noncustodial parent and become resentful if they hear negative comments or feedback. This creates a lose–lose situation for everyone.

SETTING THE STAGE 7: Spend one-on-one time with your child to maintain your relationship bond. Many people inadvertently forget about their children during the excitement of the courting stage. Sometimes this is the element that the child remembers and it causes problems between the child and their new stepparent.

Setting the stage and following these steps in whatever form works best for you and your child will make a world of difference for everyone in the new marriage. Now it's your turn to determine how you feel you can best prepare your children for your remarriage.

Keep the tips on how to prepare your children for remarriage handy by going to www.stopmarryingmistakes.com and downloading your own copy of **Preparing Children for Remarriage.**

ASSIGNMENT 75: Identify and list some of the things you will do to prepare your children for your remarriage. If you have adult children, don't forget them.

1

2

3

4

5

6

7

8

9

10

SETTING THE STAGE

SETTING THE STAGE 1: Never hide the relationship from your children.

SETTING THE STAGE 2: As your relationship progresses, involve your children in activities. You should always observe how your dating partner interacts with your children.

SETTING THE STAGE 3: Take your time. Many remarriages occur so fast that the building of the relationship bond between the child and the stepparent doesn't have time to develop. Consequently, the child doesn't trust the stepparent.

SETTING THE STAGE 4: As the relationship turns toward marriage, discuss this possibility with the child. Be open and frank. Solicit your child's opinions. Don't feel like you have to defend the person you're dating. Listen to your child's concerns without being judgmental.

SETTING THE STAGE 5: Never demand that your child has to like your dating partner. Let your child slowly engage in the relationship.

SETTING THE STAGE 6: Avoid making negative comparisons between the person you're dating and your ex-spouse. Let your child make his or her own observations.

SETTING THE STAGE 7: Spend one-on-one time with your child to maintain your relationship bond.

Preparing your child, yourself, and your future partner for remarriage is extremely important. Taking the time to do it right will be a blessing to many lives.

REFERENCES:

Pasley, K, & Ihinger-Tallman, Marilyn, eds. *Remarriage and Stepparenting: Current Research and Theory.* New York: Guilford Press, 1987.

Spanier, G. B., & Thompson, L. Parting: *The Aftermath of Separation and Divorce.* Newbury Park, CA: Sage, 1987.

U.S. National Center for Health Statistics, Marriage Rates and Median Age of Bride and Groom, by Previous Marital Status: 1970 to 1987." In Statistical Abstract of the United States, 111 ed., p. 87. Washington D.C.: Government Printing Office, 1991. Wallerstein, J. S., & Blakeslee, S. Second Chances: Men, Women, and Children a Decade After Divorce. Ticker& Fields, March 1989.

RECOMMENDED READING:

Visher, E. B., & Visher, J. S. *How to Win as a Stepfamily.* Brunner/Mazel, New York, 1991.

Conclusion

A divorce can be one of the hardest things a person will ever go through. With proper care and work, most of the negativity can be avoided or worked out. If you take time before dating to heal and learn about yourself, relationships, and life, a divorce can be the turning point that guides you on a most rewarding journey.

You can look back on it as one of hardest things you did, and also as one of the most worthwhile because of the skills and insights you've gained. You can find true joy, even after divorce, by first getting to know, believe, and value yourself, and then going on to develop meaningful relationships using the principles in this book.

You can live the rest of your life embracing the excellence that lies within every one of us.

Happy journey to excellence!

It is up to you to decide how your divorce is going to affect you and those loved ones around you.

It is up to you to decide how your divorce is going to affect you and those loved ones around you.

Charts

THE RESISTANCE / DEPRESSION MODEL:

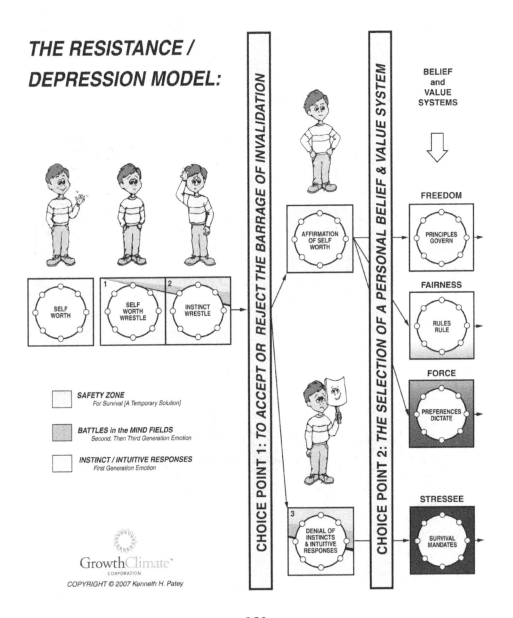

BELIEF and VALUE SYSTEMS

SELF WORTH

1 SELF WORTH WRESTLE

2 INSTINCT WRESTLE

SAFETY ZONE
For Survival [A Temporary Solution]

BATTLES in the MIND FIELDS
Second, Then Third Generation Emotion

INSTINCT / INTUITIVE RESPONSES
First Generation Emotion

CHOICE POINT 1: TO ACCEPT OR REJECT THE BARRAGE OF INVALIDATION

AFFIRMATION OF SELF WORTH

3 DENIAL OF INSTINCTS & INTUITIVE RESPONSES

CHOICE POINT 2: THE SELECTION OF A PERSONAL BELIEF & VALUE SYSTEM

FREEDOM
PRINCIPLES GOVERN

FAIRNESS
RULES RULE

FORCE
PREFERENCES DICTATE

STRESSEE
SURVIVAL MANDATES

GrowthClimate
CORPORATION
COPYRIGHT © 2007 Kenneth H. Patey

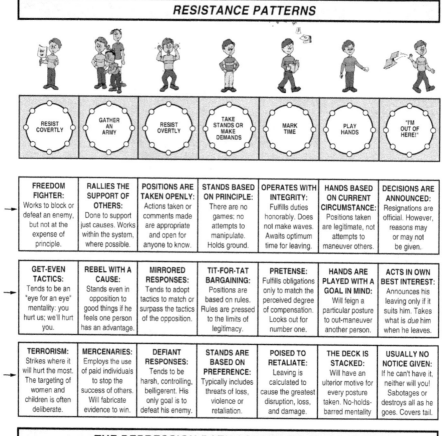

RESISTANCE PATTERNS

			TAKE STANDS OR MAKE DEMANDS			
RESIST COVERTLY	GATHER AN ARMY	RESIST OVERTLY		MARK TIME	PLAY HANDS	"I'M OUT OF HERE!"

FREEDOM FIGHTER:	RALLIES THE SUPPORT OF OTHERS:	POSITIONS ARE TAKEN OPENLY:	STANDS BASED ON PRINCIPLE:	OPERATES WITH INTEGRITY:	HANDS BASED ON CURRENT CIRCUMSTANCE:	DECISIONS ARE ANNOUNCED:
Works to block or defeat an enemy, but not at the expense of principle.	Done to support just causes. Works within the system, where possible.	Actions taken or comments made are appropriate and open for anyone to know.	There are no games; no attempts to manipulate. Holds ground.	Fulfills duties honorably. Does not make waves. Awaits optimum time for leaving.	Positions taken are legitimate, not attempts to maneuver others.	Resignations are official. However, reasons may or may not be given.
GET-EVEN TACTICS:	**REBEL WITH A CAUSE:**	**MIRRORED RESPONSES:**	**TIT-FOR-TAT BARGAINING:**	**PRETENSE:**	**HANDS ARE PLAYED WITH A GOAL IN MIND:**	**ACTS IN OWN BEST INTEREST:**
Tends to be an "eye for an eye" mentality: you hurt us; we'll hurt you.	Stands even in opposition to good things if he feels one person has an advantage.	Tends to adopt tactics to match or surpass the tactics of the opposition.	Positions are based on rules. Rules are pressed to the limits of legitimacy.	Fulfills obligations only to match the perceived degree of compensation. Looks out for number one.	Will feign a particular posture to out-maneuver another person.	Announces his leaving only if it suits him. Takes what is *due* him when he leaves.
TERRORISM:	**MERCENARIES:**	**DEFIANT RESPONSES:**	**STANDS ARE BASED ON PREFERENCE:**	**POISED TO RETALIATE:**	**THE DECK IS STACKED:**	**USUALLY NO NOTICE GIVEN:**
Strikes where it will hurt the most. The targeting of women and children is often deliberate.	Employs the use of paid individuals to stop the success of others. Will fabricate evidence to win.	Tends to be harsh, controlling, belligerent. His only goal is to defeat his enemy.	Typically includes threats of loss, violence or retaliation.	Leaving is calculated to cause the greatest disruption, loss, and damage.	Will have an ulterior motive for every posture taken. No-holds-barred mentality	If he can't have it, neither will you! Sabotages or destroys all as he goes. Covers tail.

THE DEPRESSION PATH / CLOSE-DOWN SEQUENCE

4	5	6	7	8
LEARNED HELPLESSNESS	VIOLATION OF PRINCIPLE	NON-VALUE FOR SELF NON-VALUE BY OTHERS	NOBODY CARES ABOUT ME HERE	I'M OF NO VALUE TO ANYONE

UPROOTING STRESS MODEL

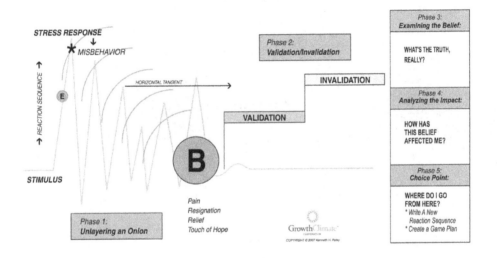

MY FAMILY BACKGROUND CHART

My Husband's Parents		My Parents	
Father	Mother	Father	Mother
Country of Origin			
Number of Children			
Occupation			
Years of Education			
Importance of Organized Religion			
Decision Maker			
Teaches/Disciplines			
Handles the Money			

About the Author

Lisa has built an award winning film and book business including eighteen books written to date. As *The Step It Up Queen,* Lisa has stepped up in her own life and has not allowed dyslexia to stop her from becoming a prolific author and following her own dreams. She is the former host of the radio program *The Hero Factor.* Lisa continues to write novels and information-packed books to educate others about successful relationships and stepping up every area of their lives. She brings the benefits of her knowledge, wisdom, and training to you through her coaching services. Lisa shares her insights with others around the world to help everyone get out of their own way and step it up to realize their potential. www.stepitupqueen.com

Do you ...

➤ Feel held back in your business, job or home life?
➤ Never dare to dream?
➤ Feel like you can't get anything done? or
➤ Procrastinate and aren't as effective as you could be?
➤ Get stuck and aren't sure how to move forward to get what you want?

Let Lisa J. Peck help you "step it up" and get what you want.

After having the courage to face her fears and break through them, Lisa J. Peck set new standards for her life and is now known as "The Step-It-Up Queen." She has inspired more than a million people with her life story and capacity to get things done.

Are you overwhelmed? Have you settled for the status quo?

As a mother of seven children, inspired entrepreneur, savvy businesswoman, passionate writer, beloved author and speaker, Lisa guides you through the steps to create an environment of accountability and support in your life.

Visit www.stepitupqueen.com

Thriving After Divorce CD Package

Lisa J. Peck steps it up and dives in deep during an in-depth twenty hour interview with Dr. Kevin B. Skinner filled with kind words, humor and loving support. She asks the tough questions that most divorcees wish they could ask.

Using Stop Marrying Mistakes as a guide post, Lisa and Kevin weave through the maze of divorce and remarriage to guide the listener with practical real life examples about how to claim the life you want. Listen to these enriching 19 hours plus a bonus CD. They will help you to stop marrying mistakes – for good.

www.stopmarryingmistakes.com

~ For 15% discount, enter in Stop Mistakes Now with purchase. ~

BUY A SHARE OF THE FUTURE IN YOUR COMMUNITY

These certificates make great holiday, graduation and birthday gifts that can be personalized with the recipient's name. The cost of one S.H.A.R.E. or one square foot is $54.17. The personalized certificate is suitable for framing and will state the number of shares purchased and the amount of each share, as well as the recipient's name. The home that you participate in "building" will last for many years and will continue to grow in value.

Here is a sample SHARE certificate:

THIS CERTIFIES THAT

YOUR NAME HERE

HAS INVESTED IN A HOME FOR A DESERVING FAMILY

1985-2005

TWENTY YEARS OF BUILDING FUTURES IN OUR
COMMUNITY ONE HOME AT A TIME

1200 SQUARE FOOT HOUSE @ $65,000 = $54.17 PER SQUARE FOOT
This certificate represents a tax deductible donation. It has no cash value.

YES, I WOULD LIKE TO HELP!

I support the work that Habitat for Humanity does and I want to be part of the excitement! As a donor, I will receive periodic updates on your construction activities but, more importantly, I know my gift will help a family in our community realize the dream of homeownership. **I would like to SHARE in your efforts against substandard housing in my community!** *(Please print below)*

PLEASE SEND ME _____ SHARES at $54.17 EACH = $ $_____

In Honor Of: _____

Occasion: (Circle One)   HOLIDAY   BIRTHDAY   ANNIVERSARY

　　　　OTHER: _____

Address of Recipient: _____

Gift From: _____   *Donor Address:* _____

Donor Email: _____

I AM ENCLOSING A CHECK FOR $ $_____ PAYABLE TO HABITAT FOR

HUMANITY <u>OR</u> PLEASE CHARGE MY VISA OR MASTERCARD *(CIRCLE ONE)*

Card Number _____   Expiration Date: _____

Name as it appears on Credit Card _____   Charge Amount $ _____

Signature _____

Billing Address _____

Telephone # Day _____   Eve _____

PLEASE NOTE: Your contribution is tax-deductible to the fullest extent allowed by law.
Habitat for Humanity • P.O. Box 1443 • Newport News, VA 23601 • 757-596-5553
www.HelpHabitatforHumanity.org

Printed in the USA
CPSIA information can be obtained
at www.ICGtesting.com
JSHW012014140824
68134JS00025B/2413

9 781600 375224